RADIATION MACHINE GUN FUNK

RADIATION MACHINE GUN FUNK

Roger Smith

THE WORD WORKS

Radiation Machine Gun Funk © 2023 Roger Smith

There
shall be no
reproduction of any
part of this book in any
form or by any means,
electronic or mechanical,
except when quoted in part
for thepurpose of review,
without permission in
writing from the
publisher.
Ask:

THE WORD WORKS
P.O. Box 42164
Washington, D.C. 20015
editor@wordworksbooks.org

Cover design by Susan Pearce based on image by Roger Wyze Smith
for Triple Wyzdym Visionz
Author photograph: Roger Wyze Smith

LCCN: 2022946774
ISBN: 978-1-944585-54-9

ACKNOWLEDGMENTS

Eternal gratitude to the editors of the following publications and venues where some of these poems, excerpts, or versions of these poems first appeared or were performed in their debut:

PRINT

Creative Outlet: "The Butchers," "Jihad Alqilam," & "I had a conversation with my daughter"

LIVE

"I thought cancer was an eyebrow-less, bald-headed Caucasian boy" live at Nuyorican Poets Café for Kraal Charles Media presents Verses in 2017, hosted by Helena Lewis.

"What if Trayvon Martin died of cancer" and "Illstreet Blues of Sheep's Clothing" live at Hudson Valley Writers Center, curated and hosted by Jennifer Franklin.

"They Change Your Name on the First Appointment of Radiation Therapy," "What if Eric Garner Was Choked Out by Throat Cancer," and "Blood Changes & Best Friends Become Strangers" live at Hellphone BK at NYC's Inspired Words series College Voices, curated and hosted by Michael Phillip Geffner.

VIRTUAL

"When the Rage Takes Over" @articulatenyc on instagram with host @presidentella.

"An Urban City" for Feature Fundraiser on instagram with host @will_allen__.

"Infamous Graffiti Murals of My Insides" on Instagram Live with host @poeticboy_d.

Monstrous love to the hosts/curators mentioned above.

I am completely grateful to my professors and mentors who challenged and pushed my thinking, writing, and revision: Kimiko Hahn, I could never thank you enough, from format to revision, to developing an eye for how things fall on the page and are read; Nicole Cooley, thank you for urging me to arm myself with my pen and face my trauma; Maaza Mengiste, for broadening my pen strokes and moniker beyond 'poet'; Roger Sedarat for reminding me performance is just as important as the writing. Super grateful to creative peers in Queens College's MFA program from 2016-2019 who have assisted in workshopping some of these poems and the earliest versions of this project and its growth into *Radiation Machine Gun Funk*, including the title.

To Nancy White and the editors, designer, and staff of The Word Works, thank you for seeing something special in my poetry and helping bring this manuscript to fruition.

Big time blessings and shoutouts to the super group of poets and writers I've bonded with over quarantine, La Cocina, for pushing my pen, my limits, keeping me in a tip top poetic form and honest to performing as well as writing. Special love to Maya Wright, Storyteller Gordon, President Ella, Goddess Iman, Symbolik Knight, Sheen Anthony, Life of Don, X the Creator, and the Wonder Twins of Poetry: Mic and Freddy. One Love.

To my Poetic Partner in Crime: Tha Real, thank you for never giving up your dreams and including me within the scope of what two similar Virgo Black husbands and fathers can accomplish if ego is never an issue and the ultimate goal is lifting the Arts and the Black community. The Malcolm and Martin Experience and Talk Dirty 2 Me have given light and life to topics of major importance in the community as well as giving a safe space for artists to shine. I'm thankful to you for the vision and the drive. We still got work to do. One Love.

Special thanks to Negus Adeyemi & Adeyemi Artistry for years of pushing Bajan artists and our talents, as well as allowing me to use my poetic gifts and branching out with a lifelong dream of giving back to the youth. Your support, influence and encouragement mean the world. One Love.

I'd be nothing without the support of my friends and family. I truly have the greatest support system in the world. This one's for Pops! One Love.

To all of the poets, writers, artists, musicians, singers and songwriters of the world, you have a voice, a word, a god-given talent, release it. You owe it to yourself, you owe it to the Most High, you owe it to those who have inspired you to turn around and inspire someone else. This thing of ours that we love is about giving back, giving hope to the youth, the next person up, and allowing our culture to shine. I pray the world gets to touch this creation of my two fears, the combination of my life's experience and trauma, dying from the inside and the possibility of being slain in these streets, a lineage from Barbados, a boy born in Brooklyn whose family moves to Queens all with Hip-Hop being the soundtrack behind it all, I pray this hits some young person's hand and eyes, and they find out that Black children can chase their creative dreams. There is a place in academia for us. I only hope that I make my mentors, my peers, and my ancestors proud, and you the reader, you the dreamer, you, looking at the pen with a thought wondering if you can do it... I'm proof that you can, now get to it.
Be strong. Love hard. Give Thanks. Repeat.

for Trinity,
    a chamber of my heart is missing without you.
        I love you past ashes.
for Daddy,
    every ounce you poured, I've guzzled
        and has made me the man I am.
for Annette,
    it's never good-bye,
        so see you later, cuz.
for my girls,
    Tarynn and Teyana,
        they'll never love you like me, but make sure they try.
for my wife
    Joy-Anne,
        fightthrueverything, always.

CONTENTS

SIDE A

"I've always been fond of the word abnormal..." . . . 7
They Change Your Name on the First Appointment of Radiation Therapy . . . 8
Hereditary Means Capable of Passing Naturally from Parent to Offspring Through the Genes . . . 10
What if Trayvon Martin died of cancer . . . 12
I thought cancer was an eyebrow-less, bald-headed Caucasian boy . . . 13
"I sit and think about the things we write" . . . 15
I Too . . . 16
"Justice, though she be blind" . . . 19
Jihad Alqilam . . . 20
"The tumultuous routine of working" . . . 23
I had a conversation with my daughter . . . 24
"The B-27 standard stationary target" . . . 25
Chronicles of the Corner: Bodega Babies . . . 26
Dear Ol' Dad . . . 29
Madagascar Hissing Cockroaches Dancing Through the Streets to Pete Rock Instrumentals . . . 31
"The comparison and contrast of cancer and gun violence" . . . 33
Inside and In-between . . . 34
Cops & Robbers . . . 35
The Butchers . . . 36
"The idea of handcuffs" . . . 39
My daughter & I had a conversation . . . 40
What If My Psychiatrist Wasn't a Stubborn Black Man Who Understands Me . . . 41
"My visions are changing" . . . 43
Waiting Rooms (A Haibun) . . . 44
Brown Leaves in the Wasteland . . . 45
"From the inception of writing these poems" . . . 46
Infamous Graffiti Murals of My Insides . . . 47

THE B SIDE

An Urban City ... 53
"I'm tired of listening to the echo" ... 56
Mávrosoma ... 57
Mávros Thánatos ... 60
"The more that people hashtag" ... 62
"I am an unapologetically black Bajan-American" ... 63
The Unseen Negro ... 64
That Thing of Ours & X-Factor Memories ... 70
Shawn Carter Correctional Facility: Inmate A112266 ... 71
"In the midst of full-stream urination it happens" ... 74
I Had a Conversation with My Daughters ... 75
"No one took it worse than my mother" ... 77
A Black Father's Final Days of Stage IV Terminal Thought-Cancer ... 78
"I stop and revisit my ancestors" ... 84
The Tail End of Rising ... 85

BONUS TRACKS

A conversation I had with my daughter ... 91
Blood Changes and Best Friends Become Strangers ... 92
The   host   Leaves ... 94
"I think about my limits and question" ... 95
"There is so much freedom in flying" ... 96
There's Manure in the Media's Wheelbarrow ... 97
Chaos on Canfield Drive: Timeline for a Body (Erasure) ... 98
"I rummaged through libraries" ... 101
The Illstreet Blues of Sheep's Clothing ... 102
What If Eric Garner Was Choked Out by Throat Cancer ... 104
"I have an oncologist for my fear" ... 106
When the Rage Takes Over ... 107

Stereotypes & The N-Word Controversy ... 110
"I heard the term cellular suicide" ... 112
Adults Don't Lie Awake Thinking About Monsters ... 113
The Act of Recurrence ... 115
On Your Mark, Get Set ... 118
I have conversations with my daughters ... 120
I had a conversation with my father ... 122
"I continue to smile, praying" ... 124

Notes ... 127
About the Author ... 127
About The Word Works ... 128
Other Word Works Books ... 129

*You may not control all the events that happen to you,
but you can decide not to be reduced by them.*

—Maya Angelou, "Letter to My Daughter"

SIDE A

I've always been fond of the word abnormal: *not normal, average, typical, or usual*; the deviation from the standard; extremely or excessively large, like my frame, my personality, and my voice, but when the anesthesiologist asks me if the doctor spoke with me about using a sedative as opposed to anesthesia because of my heart's T-abnormality, I turn cold, quiet, and regress to the recesses of my mind. I retreat somewhere between Brooklyn and Barbados. In an instant I return to the essence of myself: an unpaved street, up the gap from a bus stop in Holders Land, Bankhall, St. Michaels, Barbados. A place which Mummy says was across from Ms. Eastman's ackee tree; a colorful three-bedroom chattel house with galvanized roofing and shrubs surrounding it. A house with livestock in the back, where chickens, ducks, turkeys, pigs, and sheep huddled like family; not too far from the kitchen garden where Gran-Gran *grew she seasonings*: carrots, tomatoes, okra, peppers, scallion, thyme and all, but just a ways from the enclosed outhouse where the toilet and shower were, where Uncle Casper and Uncle Victor hightail to, to avoid lashes; or maybe I retreat to a three-bedroom apartment at 846 Prospect Place, apt. 11 to be exact, on the third floor and sit on fire escapes with my brother Ronnie, and watch teenagers who appear as giants steal bikes from kids no bigger than us, as Gran-Gran sits in the backroom watching *Young and the Restless* on a black and white television. We would sit and inhale as much of Bedford-Stuyvesant as we could, admiring the freedom of the streets that Daddy tells us were too dangerous to play in. Some weekends we would walk to Prospect Park so they could play catch, but that's not a memory, that's sedation seeping into my veins. These junctures of heritage, culture and creativity are where I migrate to on that sweltering day in August of 2011, as I lie in that *cold* room on a surgical slab while Doctor Soltani performs a biopsy on me and real-life fear and trauma highjack my life. Little did I know at the time, it would only push me deeper within the arts than I could ever imagine.

THEY CHANGE YOUR NAME ON THE FIRST APPOINTMENT OF RADIATION THERAPY

"Walk This Way" hit my ears like an 808 when Aerosmith sang
        on the Run DMC tape I jacked from my brother in '86,
electric guitar over hip-hop drums bumped
but when uttered by the nurse:
        walk this way...
the mic stand didn't break through concrete
the rocksteady of the disease did
and graffiti'd the brick barricades of my mind
        because I couldn't fathom why I'd need a radiologist.
She voices mister—I hear patient,
I hear victim, I hear sufferer, I hear blood cells gathering
        in the garage of my pelvis with rock-band intentions
instantly etching over my name on driver's license
        and Life Lock can't stop identity theft.
This nasty lump conformed inside and swallowed me whole.
How did Jonah deal in dire straits?
        because my faith is contoured to compact discs
        spinning Freaky Tah's raspy voice and the echoes
            some die with a name some die nameless;
contrarily, my chest is pumped out in a gesture of an obnoxious confidence
        ready to spurt out, "It's Mister Smith,"
but when the door opens
my voice is ambushed by ski-masked larynx
        and stifled by the fog of cold breath.
The room is a North Face arctic, the hawk is out,
my thoughts are subzero—I'm padlocked in frigidness
stiff unresponsive, an unemotional namelessness
        as if Kunta died without purpose.
The disease spray painting internally displays parallel images of
        the broken windows theorizing my environment,

like how I'm treated outside of this room.
The cells betraying my body are teaching me how to adapt to
        change
because kings are born in Bed-Stuy and migrate to Queens to
        expand kingdoms,
because culture grows on mango trees in Jackmanns and nourishes
        the dark-skinned dreamers—
Inception is realizing the nightmare within a nightmare on the first
        day of radiation,
and that *survivor* would be my new identity,
a ballroom masquerade I'd waltz through life hesitating
        to acknowledge by name,
just a fancy bowtie of health and a cummerbund hiding trauma.

HEREDITARY MEANS CAPABLE OF PASSING NATURALLY FROM PARENT TO OFFSPRING THROUGH THE GENES

Cancer is a language everyone speaks in my living room, reminiscing on my second childhood, wishing Gran-Gran could kiss my boo-boo away. I sit on couches that would become daybeds as Morpheus visits my neighborhood to sit on my eyelids. I don't know bout eternal sleep but the zzz's between the snare of my snores and the amounts of drool on my pillowcase means the sleep after radiation therapy is heaven sent.

This is the closest I've come to death, I always wake up before fading into sounds of Uncle Casper and a cough that never impedes. The cringing his wife probably made cleaning up clots of blood-infused saliva off pink and black bathroom tiles in Kensington, and how London is so far from Barbados. Two different sites of lymphoma. His neck, my groin—

The mold: wet sheets of plastic securing placement, molding body to prep for weeks of repetitious laser-lump conversations, arguments and insults shrinking the life-form inside of me. The one I didn't give birth to. Immaculately conceived cancer, every cell is here, no matter the country—

the block party effect.

My daughters will inherit my rage, my darkness, my blackness, but this, the blood...a lump—

Cancer you, cancer! My wife tells me it can now replace the F word, it's a common cuss word. It explodes into rib cages of minors in Wayanda Park like freeze tag grenades; it explodes into auditory canals of the elderly when unruly adolescents swear at one another with fingers drawn: "Freeze mother-cancer!"; it explodes into the genetic code of loved ones and plays hide and go seek behind melanin. That's what hereditary means.

I sign permission slips for my girls to go on trips or get emergency health services, not have their own blood betray them. Hereditary means capable of passing naturally from parent to offspring through the genes of Gran-Gran and Uncle Casper, and Steve and Grell Bushell, and Mummy and me, and my daughters, and my grandkids, until there's a cure, and then all we have to worry about
       is being gunned down.

WHAT IF TRAYVON MARTIN DIED OF CANCER

and George Zimmerman was his oncologist—
each chemotherapy injection, a bullet;
his IV bag filled with iced tea to cool his black tired body, bullets;
the Twin Lakes hospital gown's hood riddled with bullet-holes
that makes him the most suspicious seventeen-year-old high school threat
in a gated cancer community in which the brown swallowing him faster
        than the disease makes him unwanted.
Trayvon's hand is in his waistband because the cancer is spreading
and the itch embedded within a radiation site causes Trayvon to react;
like others of his generation, he pops skittles for pain management,
for ADHD, for depression, for the erectile dysfunction he's too young to have.
And on his head, his headphones blare "Black Steel in the Hour of Chaos" and blocks out
the fact he's followed around the ward because his cancer is dark and the deadliest, and
these assholes, they always get away, says his oncologist out of self-defense—
but his *always* should be *never*
        but is confused through the scope of a racial sniper rifle.
And tonight, Trayvon takes off running down a dimly lit hallway at 7:09 p.m.,
running from a preconceived notion that glistens when murder becomes premeditated.
The Kel-Tec PF-9 9mm semi-automatic syringe fires once—and
intracellular cytotoxic poisons explode into a teenage chest too young
to legally buy cigarettes or alcohol,
to gamble, drive, or vote—and a young boy who looks like he is up to no
        good or is on drugs or something
is dying of a disease deep in the heart
of Zimmerman's attempt to make America great—back on the cancer ward,
it's 7:30 p.m. when the drums gently roll accompanying a native Rick Ross's
        voice flowing over the autotuned of a reverberating flatline.
A seventeen-year-old patient is dying of cancer and has signed a DNR,
no one would equate this to stand-your-ground laws
but to a black boy in Sanford, Florida, it is.

I THOUGHT CANCER WAS AN EYEBROW-LESS, BALD-HEADED CAUCASIAN BOY

trying to figure out his favorite sports star to include in his make-a-wish foundation letter
while his parents search amazon.com looking for wigs for him,

the same bald-headed Caucasian boy who stares out of the window at a fake Frosty and his bullshit
top hat with a dark red buttoned nose the same color as the boy's blood-tinged mucous in
the metal waste-can next to his bed where his toy box used to be

that space is now occupied by the annoying sound of an IV machine
beeping and dripping;

all this time the Caucasian boy spent listening to Mom and Dad,
the boy giving two damns, and his parents censoring every F-bomb as if they were worse than
chemo, worse than dry mouth and the aggravating agony

of sucking ice chips and choking on prayers because the medicine killing the cancer that's killing
him is killing him too;
and the double dosage of death was ordered by his big brother, no, the doctor,
maybe the serpent or Christus Victor,
and his parents who vowed to protect him,

all they can do now is cry in his applesauce and treat him like he's handicapped,
made of fresh-fallen snow,
the one that he'll never get to make angels in,
not because death is on its way but because he no longer believes in harps,

halos and cotton-cloud wings
—and neither do I because I thought cancer didn't have an affinity to charcoal pigmentation,
the melanin within my cells would create a force field
instead of being force-fed sour patch pills that don't alleviate,

and radiation that I couldn't feel but the next day burned like oil skipping out the skillet,
itched like married cells of chicken pox and poison ivy,
and darkened like an eclipse of a young man's libido, then compelled me to shave
to match the barren patch of flesh where pubic hair had already taken leave
and I was left lethargic and over-thinking, realizing that

cancer doesn't wave a confederate flag, nor take-a-knee,
cancer doesn't pick and choose, there's no check-the-box or form to fill out,
cancer has no social media to double tap its pic or quantify likes and followers,

turns out cancer can be a bearded, black man in his early thirties with a head full of hair,
I thought
        cancer was the end of my poem—

I sit and think about the things we write towards, the topics we attack in contrast to those we fear, what we avoid. I delve deep into the recesses of my mind, and think about my wife, my children, and the ills of the world; the climate rising as young black bodies drop across America, as old black bodies crumble across the nation, as police brutality is upgraded to murder and becomes embedded in black culture, my fears are no longer just for myself. I am forced to think of my ancestors. I am forced to think of "creatures so abused and mutilated in body, so dimmed and confused by pain, that they considered themselves unworthy even of hope." These ancestors, these mothers and grandmothers that Alice Walker speaks of, are the same creatures being riddled with bullets across America now, just younger; just daughters and granddaughters. A traumatic experience that I also worry about as I raise my daughters and they grow older and search for mates to settle down with and start families of their own. A recycling of concern, and the angst reloads these headaches like machine gun turrets

I TOO

for Langston, and the Renaissance

Yeah, I kneeled—but shit, I too, sing America.

I am darker than the darker brother.
I own the kitchen in which my great-grandfather was sent to eat when company came cause
black wasn't associated with president or vice.
It was more vice than virtue,
like nigger was an apron we wore that could jump off our skin and hurt you.
Massa's house is now the name of a restaurant.
A place customers reject
cause we ain't shucking oysters or jiving turkey,
but racists are welcome—we
got the perfect jerk platter for you cause you are
what you eat… and I laugh, but under these dimples
run sewers of tears, gutters of agony,
there's even a hint of defeat in my chuckle

that Mama says gives her the chills.
Like those nights when hay wasn't for anything but hiding
and no one's horsing around. Making a sound wouldn't get you caught in hide and seek.
You'd be off to meet your maker,
the God they introduced you to,
who your ancestors do not approve cause this is not your ancestry,
no dot, no com, but the calm's in
        after your legs stopped kicking; bondage was everlasting,
blue balls of your eyes ready to pop, not a thing was erotic about
        these knots—snot ran,
as did blood,
as did our brothers and sisters,
as did our tears
and mine still do. I pray they never noticed.

I prayed they'd never know this till I was ready to share,
and now I sit here cooking, eating, growing physically strong but mentally
I'm drained.
Spiritually—well, my soul only exists, awaiting exits.

But tomorrow
I'll be cooking again. My staff out in the streets,
recruiting the hungry,
whose palate won't be distracted by the shrieks of the dead mulatto souls beneath them,
the negro spirituals on the radio, the chandeliers hung by noose,
the utensils shackled to the table or the smell of burnt flesh
chased by a curry aroma and a tinge of American history
stewed to perfection.

History of a staff of darker brothers trying to put pegs under the table and food on top
because our forefathers shaved down the wood their forefathers dangled from.
They wonder why so many of us peddle these drugs
to deviate from the reality of these cycles,
never recognizing our kick stands are tired.
No longer kicking from trees, we can't stand this shit no more.
We not pun di pond they pun.
Darker never equated to ugly little duckling.
They can't see how beautiful we are,
only how far they've "let us come."

Besides, their band-aid greenbacks are insufficient and
their full bellies intensify tears, and agony, and defeat.
I hear the feet of my great-grandfather rolling underneath these kitchen floor tiles,

kicking. Screaming I
am the darker brother wearing this
cloak of negritude as shame—trying to fit in whispering.

I too am America.

Justice, though she be blind, is a white woman with a confederate flag draped around her coke-bottled figure, reaching for a black cock to give fellatio just to have him fixed and fixated to the American dream, or nightmare pending the perception of your skin.

JIHAD ALQILAM (ÄL-KI-LÄ-MEÏ)

What if I were Muslim.
Who arises before the sun to recite portions of the Qur'an,
Bismillah hir Rahman nir Rahim.
I would make *wudhu*, washing ebony flesh
and scrubbing the American stench off my blackness,
the reek of not being accepted even before religious enlightenment,
but it remains.

I want to be a Muslim who, within my five daily prayers to Allah,
stands barefoot on sheets of
leaves of grass avoiding direct contact with native American burial grounds,
black rock and concrete slabs, skyscraper tombstones.
I'm gonna fast from the media during the month of Ramadan,
salvaging my salaam from reports of:
the hunt of niggers,
the killing of queers,
the neglect of bitches,
fasting from making America great again.

Maybe I should be a Muslim who averts holy pilgrimage to Mecca
fearing declined re-entry,
or confiscated passport,
or seizure of Baraka's "Somebody Blew Up America" in my carry on,
or worse.
Obama was born in Hawaii, and they called him
a non-citizen, non-American,
so Brooklyn must be in Syria, Iran or Iraq.
Queens, a borough etched off the coasts of Libya, Somalia, Sudan or Yemen,
each unacceptable in the die-cast melting pot.

I'm becoming a Muslim
who watches FBI agents and editors,
become simultaneous synonyms, both paid
to read between pipe bomb poetry lines.
Homeland security scans for cells and suicide,
submissions strapped to chapbooks;
tired eyes blurred from manuscripts and paper-cut fingers rummaging through pages,
searching themselves in empty rooms with two-way mirrors,
for morality, for reasons of whether or not to continue reading
or scrap paperbacks inscribed in Arabic as if the language
ticked
and exploded from the page with ball bearings and shrapnel, other than stimuli flying at readers.
Is it now a crime to make the mind ponder?
What about you?
Would you toss quills found on my desk (without warrant)
in a stack with the radicals or
slowly let the ink run dry and force me to watch
as I'm shackled and dehumanized.
No phone calls. No right to bear pens. No "in Allah we trust" printed on the back of your currency.
Go ahead and strip me of a constitutional right not written for tar-baby-turned-terrorist;
would you notice? Would you care?

I've always been "one who submits to God,"
exclusively dedicated—
like your government officials,
like your pastors, your professors,
like your parents: married to ideals,
lying to myself, stealing opportunity, killing the white picket-fenced dream by an adultery of culture,
worshipping the mixed-up mulatto starred-and-striped rape baby;
my head covered by a hijab or a turban,
will I be quarantined?

Locked up and questioned "randomly,"
held responsible for the implosion of the towers
while Bin Laden and al-Qaeda were righteously sought out and murdered
for acts carried out three days after my birthday
while I scribed unpatriotic poems and protests, making me a jihadist,
struggling, seeking refuge from the war on
humanity, the war on
liberty, the war
on freedom, written and sung for Sunni and Shia
to not understand;
infrared dot foreheads, why target a religion when hate crimes create infrastructural meltdowns
as the equivalence of prejudice and democracy grows?

I am Muslim,
and a poet,
living on freedom of speech soil that is watered down blood
of slaves, on the slabs of concrete and blacktop.
I wonder which makes me more of a threat to
the way of life of those restoring greatness.
والقلم يستمر إن شاء الله
walqalam yastamirr in shā' Allāh.

The tumultuous routine of working until you're old and gray can cause wear and tear on the mind, body and soul. The joys of family play a major role in releasing some of the stress, tension, and anxiety between paying bills and punching a clock, and still, I use writing as an escape. These routines are what we working middle-class writers get caught up in, enveloped by the mundane, busy and just existing. So for once I just stop writing and start an exceedingly important conversation with my daughters while sitting together at the dining room table where we do homework collectively. The question: what they think is a scarier way to die as a youth in America, from cancer or being shot down in the streets because of the color of their skin. It takes a bit of time for each of my children to answer, but the conversation sparked introduces me to a new critical direction to enter my research with a new emotional attachment. It raises the stakes for me and makes the writing more personal. It's no longer just about me and my ordeal but my girls and the future of my family. Generational trauma.

I HAD A CONVERSATION WITH MY DAUGHTER

about the differences between
having cancer and being black in America,
and she told me that cancer is black, dark, dismal and causes depression,
blackness in the brain, to the core of the central nervous system,
it metastasizes, and the people in their angelic lab coats,
the ones wielding MD as a knight does his shield,
take an oath to help you, plug you up to the matrix and damn near kill you, in every valiant
effort they can to accomplish what they said they would—whereas
being born black in America, young men are detached
from success's outlet so kinetic vigor bleeds into the streets
and potential is buried in the system
or in a booth, both behind bars
with bantam opportunity. The cords that lead to tomorrow
are severed by the trajectory of metallic fragments
spewed from semiautomatic odium,
panic muzzled behind law and a sniper-rifled rage which causes brain matter to overflow;
furthermore, the people in the glacier-blue uniforms who possess the title officer
hide behind shield, ignore the oath to serve and protect,
squeeze abnormal amounts of munitions to achieve their very first kill; the
    depression and gloom are watermarks of perception—cancer
        produces hope.

The B-27 standard stationary target used by law enforcement with a black silhouette is 24" x 45" and costs 89¢ per sheet, but the moving ones in the street with various heights and weights are free. I suppose target practice is saving tax payers money while eliminating the darker non-taxpayers.

The standard magazine capacity for a Smith and Wesson .40 caliber Glock 22 is 15 rounds; one would imagine that upon reloading a warning shot is an afterthought.

CHRONICLES OF THE CORNER: BODEGA BABIES

to the mother of the black boy that got his rights violated last night around the corner from the reader

from birth she baptized her baby
    in a blend of acid water and bleach
to bathe off the black that attracts bullets
    from badge wearers who blind crowds with blue words
        like *serve and protect*,
sirens blare at the hours when only doom lurks on blacktop,
    when bodegas bolster doors, so
bulletproof windows receive the barrage of orders
    of chopped cheese, and burgers with bacon
never broiled, tossed on besmirched flattops
    beggars become blatant—as the sizzling begins:

He was only at the Ahks for eleven minutes to order a sandwich and try to settle the stomach grumblings that come with post radiation and the nothings in the fridge at home
    burgers with bacon on besmirched flattops
his mother is absent because she works all day and night to provide for her children who are fatherless because the system that is ultimately allowing marijuana to be legal said it was illegal to smoke and carry all but ten years ago.
    from birth she baptized her baby and bathed off the black
He's famished from debate and basketball practice and helping his siblings with homework, so he walked around the corner where everyone who looks like him sells drugs, or guns, or both, and
    woop woop!
officers hop out of paddy wagons with loud voices and ears tucked away, hands on weapons, on nightstick, on gun, on taser, attitude and aggression on a thousand, words on violent and vulgar, and demands of on the ground, of hands up, of mouths closed, on where's the shit at? on whatcha'll out

here so late for? on pat 'em down, on feel his chest, on why you so nervous, on where you think you going, nigguh—
and the sizzling...
The questions could only be rhetorical as pockets are emptied, cellphones tossed on the curb, wallets pulled, any IDs confiscated to run names through databases that would only confirm ghetto black intent, rather caucasian cop knowledge taught at the academy
from badge wearers who blind crowds with blue words
and the other youngins mouth off but he kneels in silence, in fear, in a realization that this could be his last night, in playing catch with his mother who couldn't throw a ball for shit, in helping her eat after the mastectomy, in helping his little sister write Father's Day cards they never sent, in praying he could get a cell besides his father's because a casket was more realistic .
the blots, blood, and bullet casings on the blacktop
He recalls the things his father used to say like wrong place, wrong time always leads to worst place for a long time; or advice in dealing with the boys in blue, Grin and bare it, baby boy... no sudden moves, when they call you boy and shove you around just grin, and bare it, it was like he and his father were back at home on a rundown couch catching up on lost time and words without glass between them
in a blend of acid water and bleach
in the heat of summer of two thousand and
the sizzling
of his brain not being able to remember the year or stay present in this moment, discomfort disrupts him, his body betrays him and he moves— key the sounds we wish are firecrackers but during confrontations between flatfoots and bodega babies, are not

as the sizzling began
    the blemishes of blood and bullet casings
from badge wearers who blind crowds with blue words
    like *serve and protect,*

bubbled on the boulevard where a mother can now barely breathe,
      can't read *goodbyes* from the baby boy she birthed and baptized
in a blend of acid water and bleach
      just to bathe off the black that attracts bullets
she buries her remaining babies in what
      once was her bosom and buries her burdens
           within herself.

DEAR OL' DAD

> *inspired by the Rudy Francisco excerpt on Instagram:*
> *Racism is the drunk guy at the party*
> *who tries to fight everyone.*
> *America says nothing*
> *and pretends*
> *they didn't ride*
> *in the same car.*

To go further, Rudy, America is racism's father,
no, the cool dad
that tells him it's okay to drink like this
and exhibit these true colors

since rainbows are now accepted.
When change is
on the rise

like confederate flags waving on windy evenings,
when indictments of crooked cops, no,
crooked men equivocates colored privilege—
I apologize, when people who are paid to protect

weren't trained properly
and *mistake* black people as the silhouettes
on their pages of practice, so they fire—which
comes first,

the intent to kill black folk or the badge?
America
is racism's cool dad that smokes pot with
him and pays for his first tattoo

of ah three-dimensional swastika,
ah bald eagle, and ah noose,
to match the ink imprinted on his cerebellum,
walls that read superiority

but sound stupid at every party.
He finds himself doing lines of cocaine
to drown out finding that black girl cute
and further tunes in with corroded

thoughts of rape that would make
his father proud and blind any shroud
of being different. America is racism's dear ol' dad
who keeps his foot on his son's throat,

just to feel great again.

MADAGASCAR HISSING COCKROACHES DANCING THROUGH THE STREET TO PETE ROCK INSTRUMENTALS

It was the roaches
   or so I thought,
the reason diaspora meant pack
   suitcases, accents, and smacks with cou-cou
stick and leave Bed-Stuy in the rearview,
   but Mummy knew the real reason was because
hard-ears children would stand on Nostrand Ave
   with targets on back, on chest,
on future because all black boys wearing hoodies
   grow into felons who deserve cages
or closed caskets before they get to *straighten it out*.
   See, parents of black teenagers don't worry
about suicide or bullying,
   but bullets turning brown bodies into bulletins
pinned to a hashtag or a T-shirt
   or the words rest-in-peace graffitied on storefronts
when *they reminisce over you*.
   That's a fear Daddy passed down to me,
   it's the reason text messages
are minutes in front and seconds behind curfew
   while I'm in front of the house
behind the wheel looking for my oldest daughter
   when she's minutes late.
Fragments of possibility scatter like roaches
   when the lights of a squad car
illuminate the malevolence of midnight,
   never shining on the unseen negro,
never shining on *Mecca or the soul brother*
   just gunshots and bullet sounds when we
attempt to stay calm or beat box

  to reduce the anxiety my slang may cause any officer,
just more possibilities of danger buried in this
  skin tone of ours attached to
a false hatred for law enforcement, for authority,
  from ancestors stolen and beaten
like a shoe hovering over a roach in a world which
  you thought *was yours*—
a history of drowning while wading yet we're told to forget it
  and it's so damn hard cause we're still spitting up
debris from the Ohio River and our wrists still pain us
  but that don't compare to the constant staring
down the barrel of a glock 17 *baby pa*,
  and the deafening silence of a burning pinch
in your chest, so deep that you feel the warm
  air exit your back as you struggle
to inhale blood bubbling air and everything
  above you darkens,
this is the freedom stitched to the banner yet waving
  Moor residue at the bottom of a leather oxford.

The comparison and contrast of cancer and gun violence covers a large percentage of deaths of black people nationwide and deserves to be discussed in every genre of literature. Police gun violence, which is usually racially perpetuated, is a type of cancer also spreading across America; and in reverse as cancer spreads through the body, organs burst as if the projectiles that hit them explode, but from the inside. Pop Quiz: who are you more afraid of, them or yourself?

INSIDE AND IN-BETWEEN: AN ABECEDARIAN

Air* has a way of moving through the
body, in-between bones, around arteries and
closely connecting to the norm, but
different.
Everything inside
flows as it should, except for this, this
group of cellular confusions that
hover in the system's no-fly zone. The
itching is ignored or speculated as
just a simple rash. Nothing that
keeps the mind's attention. Showers are not meant to find
lumps or
masses or
nodes that decide to implode of their
own accord. You haven't signed
permission slips for reckless parties or okay'd
quantum increases inside your insides.
Rarely are we even aware, or brought into the
seamless fold as
tragedy multiplies and spreads. The superficial has
unnoticeable trauma but is sometimes still
visible. Underneath the cowl you
wear, treatment or prolonging takes its toll and
X-rays and pet scan after ct scan after poking and prodding you,
you want so badly to quit, but you're almost done. Almost through the
zigzags, the fatigue, the ribbons, the dying on the inside.

> * When cops replace 'air' with bullets, they travel the same but some may find it a harder task to resuscitate the unarmed black body, lying there, dying in between the high-fives.

COPS AND ROBBERS

I always begged to be a robber.
I would put on a Zorro mask for disguise
because as a school-aged child I knew we all look
like target practice posters moving back and forth
but in real time with guns that shoot back.
True fear was getting arrested
and being locked up to a chair in the mango-scented living room
that Aunty Cora said not to disturb. Still I knew
I'd always side with the robbers so I would hide in the shadows
of a twelve-noon rising-middle-class brownstone in Brooklyn
plotting on snagging sardines from a cabinet I couldn't reach
while my brother radioed in any activity he heard
from the slightly light plantain-tinted kitchen
on the Dixie-cup scanners attached by cord while our cousin Andrew sat on the other side,
then I slipped by trying not to shake beaded curtains at the doorway
separating unlimited now-a-laters from hours of nuggies—
a bulky Sony Walkman was weighing down my husky wrangler jeans,
but its cheap foam earpieces bumped words of the message that would resonate
years later when I thought about the side I never chose,
it's like a jungle sometimes it makes me wonder how I keep from going under-
neath the mask or the uniform to the nucleus of the person.
The losses didn't leave carcasses in my godmother's dining room
or my body dangling in a back room closet from a hefty bag
no DNA trails of unanswered questions from parents about botched broughtupsy
and winning wasn't compensated leave for executioners.

THE BUTCHERS

> *Most young kings get their heads cut off.*
> *—Jean Michel Basquiat*

1.
They mistook sun-grilled flesh for Neanderthals,
beastly because bars and chains
can't cage humanity.
Buried babies and burnt bodies cloaked a culture
under mountains, under tundra.
They never saw people, just seared meat.

Lights on, tickets pulled, victims stand on line
to be called in succession
but never see past tools of execution.
The truth of butchers, hiding behind carcasses,
hands on the block,
his life's work spilled all over. Soul, as stained as uniform.

Pitch-black provisions scaled down
to charred molecules
with perfect precision,
trained well in the academy to cut down kingdoms.
Cubes, cylinders, and
the substance of things hoped for reduced
to chunks of muddled meat.

Basquiat's brush beat canvas in the multi-
cultural hallucination
of the Lower East Side in the 80s.
Ironic enough, black butchers.
There's money between the scales of God, Law.
Duffle bags of dead men

as simony for souls chopped down.
Vanished...
those species, those tribes,
those peoples, those nations,
those kingdoms.
Zulu, Maasai, Dinka, Ashanti, San Bushmen:
gone, goodbye, and good riddance.

2.
Ding!
Back to the blacktop beefed-up section, to Jean-Michel and the obnoxious liberals,
to four-digit, shiny gold-badged licenses to kill,
to necrophilia resembling stop and frisk before
the liberated bullet leapt,

to splatter the colors within beasts
on gravel explicating life.
How is history discharged on canvas?
Is it a sound rupturing the midnight air,
is it a scorched hole left in flesh,
or possibly the oozing and smearing
of blood on a cutting board?

Open the cages of your ribs. Carve out
that repulsive *ngoma*,
feel the thumping cries of the hunt
between your fingers as the hunger pangs amplify
and that banner yet waves.

Mother, have you tired of obsidian?
Are the mathematics of the pyramids lies?
Is the Nile tarnished?
Why has the melting pot become a wrought iron skillet, and the employment of butchers intensified?

The butchers, tools holstered at their side,
no longer an object of omnipresence
who would occasionally hack an irrational animal.
The butchers,
paid to slaughter without question or instruction,
without limitation,
endangering all sun-bathed species,
internally entering their own murkiness.

The idea of handcuffs is parallel to the representation of chains during slavery; so after sensitivity training, the decision to shoot black males is a much more delicate way to handle the matter.

                 handcuffs   represent
slavery; so   shoot black males

I watched a movie last night and 41 shots took down a robot. I know blacks are considered magical, but robots?

MY DAUGHTER AND I HAD A CONVERSATION

about cancer and blackness in America and she expressed concerns about
love—about never finding a boyfriend whose hoodie isn't riddled
with holes of racial profiling; about being an innocent spectator as she awaits
a kiss; about lymphoma heirlooms and being on a metal slab
next to a boyfriend—chemo running her veins, shrapnel running his;
about Daddy being gunned down and cancer
seeping into the cross island; about reaching for her cellphone at the wrong time; about
     reaching in her purse at the wrong time; about reaching out;
about reaching;
     about having conversations with her sisters about what happened to Daddy
for reaching for the gun he didn't have and that he was only trying to
     scratch the radiation site when they emptied all clips,
         then reloaded,
             then continued to fire,
             then continued to fire,
                to fire,
                     fire.

WHAT IF MY PSYCHIATRIST WASN'T A STUBBORN BLACK MAN WHO UNDERSTANDS ME

My brother is washing dishes with my oldest daughter,
it's evening and the sun is beginning to set.
I put four ice cold .45 ACP hollow points at the bottom of my glass
and poured three fingers of Gentleman Jack, then toast
to my oncologist to whom I attribute saving my life seven years ago
and who has died today from pancreatic cancer. In
our last conversation she advised "Roger, go abroad, and visit
        third-world countries where race isn't important" on Thursdays
because the bellies of twelve-year-olds have been vacant
        since Monday.
My wife is going over my youngest daughter's homework as the rest of
        us migrate from the dining room table.

        My psychiatrist sneaks in and tells me I'm deflecting but
          I rarely listen to what a mirror says back.

Split-personality disorder is not an inherent gene in my family but *on the*
        ledge tête-à-têtes are—
Cancer however is a language everyone speaks in my living room
        though we venture from different avenues;
Mummy talks loud in a multiple myeloma type gibberish that drowns out
my recurrent patois,
        Uncle Casper's late Hodgkin's Creolese whispers from
        the urn on the mantle.
When we change subjects to being gunned down because of the color of
        our skin,
it's a nasty vernacular which Daddy takes the lead touching
        on youth, age, respect, and compliance,
so fault lingers as the lingo runs parallel to the manure the media has
        revised our lives with;
            bullets and black tumors.

Door bells and oven beeps, cellphones ringing mesh
with radiation machines and machine gun funk; it's all noise, everything is
noise and I love it because silence is the deafening feeling of the
cold running your veins;

"And how does that make you feel" my psychiatrist utters

it's the lab rat metallic table, or the mold around your thighs and ass keeping you in place;
it's chemotherapy cleansing humanity as it's calling my complexion
cancer;
it's the shrieks from parents of teenagers lying on concrete slabs in
America's war zone;
it's dark-skin suspiciousness; it's mammograms to mulattoes who thought
they escaped;
it's a central venous catheter to a redbone swimsuit model;
it's the what-ifs;
it's the conversations with my daughter about doctor visits and check-ups
and boyfriends and making sure they're not assholes during
interactions with badged assholes;
it's the ever-so-often CT scans and the blood work, the wait,
the too much weight gain versus the too much weight loss;
it's trying to fall asleep before anyone else does to avoid thinking about it,
avoid talking about it, avoid writing about it—

The living room is clear now. I'm alone
in a darkness like me
with my psychiatrist again chirping

You're making headway. I think now would be a good time for another session

I take a sip—still *cold*, I haven't used ice in a drink at home since the night
I was called with my diagnosis.

My visions are changing, transforming, developing with more intimate thought every time I read something new or old. There's an intense involvement between myself and the text, I'm remixing the information, blending it with innovative language and creating pieces that I have never imagined. I'm engaging with the cancer as well as my blackness at simultaneous instances instead of attacking them as individual fears, thus releasing their stronghold over my mind, and now nothing is more urgent than sharing it with the world. These exact thoughts are encapsulated by Lorde as she states, "we become more in touch with our own ancient, black, non-european view of living as a situation to be experienced and interacted with, we learn more and more to cherish our feelings, and to respect those hidden sources of our power from where true knowledge and therefore lasting action comes." As the weight is discharged from my past's chamber, I enter true freedom through language and literature, watching my trauma hit the cement like a thousand shell casings.

WAITING ROOMS (A HAIBUN)

The women clench their expensive purses. Pull their children in ... closer, as if body heat protects them and the blackness crawling my skin may infect them. These masks are nothing new to them. Eyes are diverted from candies crushing on screens and abrupt pauses in any dialect, shouts of discomfort. White men with empty seats besides them instantly get fatter or realize their newspaper has a sudden shortness of breath and needs to sit for a sec. No vacancy. No subtlety, blatancy is saliva spewing in the eye with vicious intent. The toxic liquid I'm dragging next to me glows as it streams to a PICC line in a dark arm. The nurse placed a cape on the IV bag as I have asked. Toddlers point at the attraction, as if this super fluid will save my life, while their parents tackle their little fingers and shrink behind fake chuckles and scared smiles. CNN reports more follies at 1600 Pennsylvania Avenue. The president is worse than the coronavirus but the fear of contagion rallies in the story of my pigment. I'm reading their expressions. Some still get shocked at America's greatness again—others, however, keep me in their line of sight, peripheral at the least. After all, I am the more imminent danger: the cancer patient—the darker brother.

> Strangers fill a room.
> Blackness and cancer walk in,
> which makes them cringe first?

BROWN LEAVES IN THE WASTELAND

Owls reside in Queens. In morbid trees with jaundiced leaves committing suicide and
    spinning to their end,
somersaulting as they wither away in mid-air, wind at their backs, ignoring the hoots.
In the distance, they wait for Allah to arrive and return them to the Earth, plant it
    amidst seeds and watch it rejuvenate,
reappear, be reborn as a rose bush
full of thorns—full of color, the moon illuminates its path while leaving
the barks of canines surrounded by shadows and alley cats fighting the brisk weathers of November.
Venetian blinds whisper to be attentive,
to raise antenna and listen,
past sirens and vrooming embedded in the cross-island listen
to the bells of Prince of Peace Lutheran Church and the sweet sounds of revival and lies.
There's a howl to find serenity in,
something as sacrilegious as the strumming C-sharp of a .38. Crickets.
Phukking crickets always interfere, and as anger bubbles, the system begins influx:
of nocturnal flank affliction,
of fatigue with its heavy backside weighing on eyelids, and posture fails,
tattoos turn to hopscotch boxes as shoulders become slabs of concrete
    anchoring towards the radiator, your
soul longs to feel the warmth since your mind commits to the cold.
Week one of radiation is over and you remember you don't believe in reincarnation,
in the oneness of things,
that nature is a beautification of science and God is inept.
Your insides are brown leaves in the wasteland where owls become vultures,
the moon never knew you and the silence is picking at your flesh.

From the inception of writing these poems and putting things together they begin to liberate me. Rather than continue to repress the trauma within, I am turning this energy into a collection of deliverance simply by allowing my pen to help work through my mind. Audre Lorde claims, "Our poems formulate the implications of ourselves, what we feel within and dare make real ... our fears, our hopes, our most cherished terrors." My fears have given way to my hopes. Every piece I work on breaks a new brick. I expect to walk over rubble that was once a wall. My most cherished, uncanny terrors are being attacked, opening new possibilities for future writing that will allow my voice to represent a larger percentage of black culture.

INFAMOUS GRAFFITI MURALS OF MY INSIDES

It's funny how certain words don't have the same meanings after cancer—

cold becomes a room of silence with metal slabs and scientists running fuh
        exit signs, a place you'd imagine the first Terminator being created
as you turn looking fuh John Connor or to hear Schwarzenegger's voice;
        your breath is visible and spells out fear, but tomorrow is an
        ellipsis transitioning into a question mark, there's a green beam
        eating away at the outer epithelial layers of your skin,
flesh burnt, my groin smells like overcooked ribs,
bbq sauce scorched onto foil such that mitochondria develop grave
        markers for hair follicles.

survivor: is that what I am? So it's not the kid with a 72.4 average that
        knew college was overpriced beer pong tournaments with a
        plethora of unprotected sex,
an abundance of F's on papers about dead white authors who were
        tertiary in comparison to Baldwin, Wright, Ellison,
and commuting to and from a technologically advanced campus with
        more intelligent hobos strolling by or playing hacky sack than
        actually attending;
said kid signs up for two tours in Iraq and *comes back* alive with both
        arms, no legs and can't stand himself—but I'm the survivor?

Site or *cite* or *sight*:   Mind still translates to groin like
What a (right inguinal radiation) sight to see or cite your references: chafed flesh,
raw and swarthy, 2011 edition, NY, pages—rather age 31; apply Eucerin
to the site three times a day
to decrease irritation,
        diminish itching,
                or risk scratching to the white meat—

I return to the cold itch site—these hallways of my pelvis
which look like an 80s subway car out of Electric Boogaloo.
Each partition plastered in *Wild Style* and *Blockbuster* fonts.
                                      Each tag a different doctor
utilizing arrows, curves, and spikes pointing to words with new meanings, new places within.
These foyers of my body are art. My shrink calls it trauma.
I walk north where cells travel to an abdomen that corn meal and boiled
        okra couldn't settle, Mummy's *cou-cou* wouldn't stop me from
            feeling me cuckoo.
I see remixed Mobb Deep lyrics etched in the rubble,
                there's a war going on inside *no man is safe from;*
                you cuh run but you can't hide forever from these
                cells *that we done took—*
                                      I'm shook,
overwhelmed by the walls deteriorated by lymphoma
        and the blood cell riots of 2011,
I regurgitate myself brick by brick until I escape Hodgkins dwellings and
        notice

how funny it is that certain words don't have the same meanings after
        cancer;
laughter is an ambulance zipping down the Cross-Island Parkway
        to save a black boy's life when a gun-shot hollows his chest
            cavity allowing you to wave to his spine from an anterior view;
writing becomes therapy fuh PTSD poet churning out pages dripping
        with chemo-ink, helps wash the walls while Gran-Gran urges me to
put ah lil' elbow grease in it nuh
                        to support scrubbing away the residual
though the panorama has scars of malignant slogans and excess spray-
        painted carcinoma initials permanently etched;

trauma is a cookbook with fragments of my ancestors passed down as
 memorabilia with recipes fuh perseverance;
trauma is a photo album of answered S.O.S. signals when the corridor
 lighting fails and depression grasps a carbon black Liquitex
 aerosol can, and my shrink is unavailable.

I remember there
 ain't no such thing as halfway crooks, scared to death, scared to look—
trauma is a mural with dark shading, precision outlines, and rambunctious
 colors that throw Mike Tyson haymakers at the innocent;
trauma is a graffiti'd masterpiece I couldn't open ecchymosis eyes and
 accept.
I've been dying since diagnosis, hanging my insides at the MOMA or a
 brick wall building somewhere in Queensbridge.

THE B SIDE

AN URBAN CITY

after Charles Bukowski's "a poem is a city"

a poem is an urban city filled with broken glass and broken people
filled with hatred, stereotypes, dreams deferred, and cancer
filled with corroded cells and death
filled with coronavirus, empty carcasses in cells, and depth
    that those petty pretty posh poets never get.
a poem is an urban city filled with bloody noses and aches and pains
    and periods of pleasure,
plus periods that stop men from the hidden treasure
    chest buried within a woman's thighs. a poem
is an urban city at war, a poem is an urban city with questions the youth
    can't ask, can't answer, don't have the access to search for
    with extinct library cards,
Siri and Alexa on same-sex dates and no availability, and ultimately
    unlimited data has limitations.
a poem is an urban city pressured to try new things.
a poem is an urban city caught in the middle of see-something-say-something
    and a me-too movement that doesn't factor in crying wolf
be he big and bad, huffing and puffing,
or dressing up as Grandma, cross-dressed, transitioning or any other
gender roles or assumptions the outside world may have.
a poem is an urban city being sexually harassed, being touched inappropriately,
    being raped,
dirty fingernails and decrypted penises defiling
virgins and vaginas, vagabonds feeding on
a stanza of an urban city being body-shamed or victim-blamed
its liquor stores are half full,
its laundromats half empty, its lounges no longer exist.
Chinese food and pizzerias at every other slot,
and I don't care about what Target and Walmart got,
a poem is an urban city where everything's sold at the bodega.

a poem is an urban city where
> God streaks and his disciples bang gavels and throw pies and tomatoes at his enlarged body parts debating the authenticity of girth and length,

a poem is an urban city where raccoons are jealous of humans in their masks
at night stealing food from neighbors, from garbage can, from laborers in their own
pursuit of happiness, a poem is an urban city of poets,
all of them bitter, all of them better than the next,
but still hating everything they themselves produce
slamming into each other
not realizing they're distorting the next message
sorta like a text message...so

translations and interpretations are rendered useless
if you're using this gift wrong;
a poem is an urban city, not the slums, not the gutters
where you speak protection with words that cut her,
our Queens, our Goddesses
our Kings and Gods.
a poem is an urban city where we barely recognize the royalty within
> one another, and the walls of our kingdom

are white-washed with the brainwashing that pinpoints us
> in directions against the next

listen—a poem is this urban city here,
in the midst of nothing,
where it's 12 noon,
soaked in perspiration and emission of alcohol,
no acquitted murderers with shield, no fists of color raised to the sky,
this poem, this urban city has its doors barricaded,
multi-bolted shut,
unapologetically remorseful, aged in egotism.

reinforced steel buildings where the sun is an old wives' tale,
dark rivers of pollution and tar
        are puddles under our children's eyes.
a moon hidden by ganja smoke and hypertension,
music drowns in outstanding bills and regret,
and love—love looks like people who stand on stages or write books
or host, and ghosting becomes unfollowing poets
who slip up and exhibit imperfections
and no one's pointing fingers, we just protecting our own energies
but these entities don't realize that
a poem is an urban city, a poem is a country,
a poem is a planet, and though we ain't plan it,
we were birthed with these seeds so plant it,

sprout your existence in the midst of existing within this,
locked in some writing space
for an editor to nitpick and pick apart.
try not to rot
like an age-old apple plucked from a tree we weren't supposed to touch
that grows through the concrete in an urban city called Brooklyn—
where no one notices its beauty
and small minds ponder wicked ways to make change.
look inside of yourself and rewrite your life,
stop being the poet or the pen writing it, dying as ink bleeds into suburban streets where you don't belong.

I'm tired of listening to the echo of sonless mothers cry out as tears rain down on worthless prom tickets and cap and gown with no one left to wear them.

MÁVROSOMA

    Gk. origin mávros: *meaning black,* oma: *pertaining to marked growth; tumor.*

Finally, a *young black male* kneels.
His body tightens.
    His hands behind his back, no,
above his head!
    Fleeting above his head,
but clasped mentally in prayer.
Eyes wide shut.   Fear is a dry, unknown mass
stuck in Tar Baby's throat—
    as he swallows thinking it's the last time.

The cellphone video shows
    he is pulled and kicked.
He doesn't flinch.
He is dragged and slapped,
    coughs but doesn't flinch.

When he spits blood from out of his mouth,
    it splatters on officer 4-9-3-11's shoe.
The *black boy* apologizes and says
"Must be the cancer."

You damn right you're a cancer! 4-9-3-11 asserts.

Small blunders have tombstone results.
He is pushed and punched,
doesn't flinch.
Kicked repeatedly and spit upon.
Never flinches.

Hands now clutched behind his head,
the *boy* begins to mumble a prayer Pop Pop taught him.
      His eye expels a tear, which runs

down his face like Usain Bolt in the 100m,
      the same manner these six officers run down on him,
four pale and two brown officers in oceanic blue
sprint to surround him
      like Barbados
simply because a Caucasian lady said

"It was a young brown boy in fancy sneakers and a black T-shirt, no, a hoodie with big headphones and that loud bee-bop nonsense..."

The *target* coughs again.
                      Coughs up blood.

Officers 6-5-1-18 and 8-1-20-5 approach a young
brown lady recording everything
and that's the finale of visual footage captured
with patrol voices telling her to

"Put it away, put it away now or you're going to jail too!"

and expressions fade,
              every sound is devoured by
a clap of thunder,
      acts of ignoring a taser,
lyrics of gone too soon dedication raps
the drumbeat of Ethiopia slightly mixed
      with New York City woodwinds of not belonging.

The victim's mother cries rivers of A-student and community-giving teen
    and her love for him ricochets off parked cars
    and a-hundred-and-forty-year-old trees.
His father holds her up like piles of the Brooklyn Bridge
    with semi-soggy supportive arms,
a face aging every second as his worst nightmare plays out
he releases a trembling murmur denying all allegations
    of gang association,
of all deconstruction tools the media pitches
of toxicology report and substances found on the scene
    that desecrate the memory of their sophomore collegiate son,
    then he reiterates his good upbringing.

A nurse recognizes the assailant's body wheeled in
    with a single GSW to the frontal lobe
and her mouth opens as wide as the hole in a nineteen-year-old cranium
    which parents gaze through and read the letters never found on the scene.
Over her sobs the nurse mutters that
    the *patient* was
        "strong and sweet; a quiet soul battling stage 3 stomach cancer."
He wasn't scared of anything but every time
the needle approached him for treatment

He flinched.

MÁVROS THÁNATOS

Plague-like verdicts of acquittals, of not guilty chokeholds, of bootlegged
       wholesale cigarettes, of accusatory paraphernalia with breaking radio silence with
shouts of *shots fired!*
                             and then the failed body cam.

Maybe they thought they were in the Garden.
Badges read 23, or 24, maybe 8—Officer Jordan, LeBron or Kobe
thus they felt the need to drop
forty-one in competition with fifty,
Diallo and Bell
       couldn't hold 'em on the blacktop court so

the remainder muted protestors who march for
       the Jena Six, for the Central Park Five and when they see us
even more now; harder to claim unseen negro just
       viewed as these black rats,

not as having rights, equity or equality,
our hand out to shake for accomplishments they see as
wanting handouts so they poison us with projectiles
toss government cheese through urban mazes,
pass the nooses, and the threats, and the superpredators incarcerated while
childless mothers squall and fatherless daughters read textbooks through
       tear-infused eyes and dilapidated hands,
where ashes to ashes seep into the abyss, and voice is empty though
       mouth full of
coughed-up scraps of pan-African flags,
black fists crumbled and memories of bubonic precincts splashing,
       dancing on stars tattooed on body parts torn open

as if flesh was plastic. As if organs held microphone and the beat was about to drop,
they say niggaz love to perform.
Are these your racist jokes as black bodies gather on the news?
Candles and hashtags collage on the corner,
the black top is now a crimson-stained airbrush cenotaph.

The more that people hashtag black lives matter, the more metal shards prove to us they do not. So while you put them on your hoodie, police officers have meetings voting on the usage of bullets to play Tic-Tac-Toe.

I am an unapologetically black Bajan-American, and this—this is for a culture and lineage of blacks who are targeted, of blacks whose blood betrays them, of blacks who have dreams and gifts but don't find time to write, of blacks who don't know what an MFA program is, and for blacks who don't believe the things they write are worthy of existing in a world that despises them because of the color of their skin, their West Indian vernacular, or their indigenous slang. The lessons of education, the literature available to me from childhood to adulthood, the authors who have most influenced me, the rappers and the producers. Hip-hop has to be the soundtrack of this project as well as my life. Brothers beat-boxing while b-boys breakdance and of course the sisters are there; and not just watching, partaking in spitting razor sharp lyrics; and there's a band, an orchestra, and a choir performing with every kick and snare of my existence. Hip-hop to me is like jazz to Langston Hughes, it's "one of the inherent expressions of Negro life in America; the eternal tom-tom beating in the Negro soul—the tom-tom of revolt against weariness in a white world, a world of subway trains and work, work, work; the tom-tom of joy, and laughter, and pain swallowed in a smile." It's also the lyrics that stay with me in my most secluded and anxious times, fused with these overwhelming concerns of being a black, married, working-class man, raising three daughters in America; wondering what's gonna be the last song on my playlist?

THE UNSEEN NEGRO

> *When they approach me they see only my surroundings, themselves, or figments of their imagination—indeed, everything and anything except me.*
> —*Ralph Ellison's* Invisible Man

I am not as you see me, as they see me,
as the world sees me.
Only at a deviated altitude can one visualize
the separation from humanity,　　　step out of my darkness
open your eyes and tell me,
which came first, the monkey,

　　　　　　　　　　　orangutan
　　　　　　　　　　　　　　ape,
　　　　　　　　　　　　　　　　　gorilla—
　　　　　　　　　　　　　　　　　　　　　or the black man?

I am my blackness but it doesn't define me
I leave fingerprints on charcoal but it doesn't define me
I am in sync with the broken windows theory but that—doesn't define me.

I am a P
　　　　O
　　　E
　　　T,
　　　　　non-linear.　　　Hetero
　　　　　　　　　　　　　　　　but　s　　ed.
　　　　　　　　　　　　　　　　　　　\　/
　　　　　　　　　　　　　　　　　　　kew

　　　　　　　　　　　Consumed by my
blackness,
　　　　　　　　　　　　drowning
drowning,　　　　　　　　　　　　　　　　　　drowning
　　　drowning—
　　　　　　　　　　　　drowning.

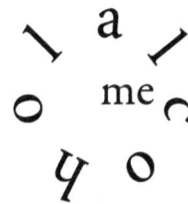

like water to an island
that refills ball point cartridge with whiskey

                                                                                            cognac,

              rum,

                                        brandy,

    bourbon,
disorientation from dark liquor then
dissemination of dark-skinned thoughts,
disambiguate the disappointment and disbelief of
the disaster this nation disguises with a term:
                            African-American.

                                                  What does it mean?
Being of two continents, two worlds, like human-martian?
    Research Africa.
    Revisit America analyzing one's self, then
                          write until melanin is regurgitated.

Light up! Recognize the generational scars of branding,
    resist, pick up a book— revolt,
    pick up a pen, break the mold,
                                    and set this shit ablaze!

Define black:
    lacking hue or brightness;
    depicted by the absence of light;
    soiled or stained with dirt;
    gloomy, pessimistic, dismal,

harmful, sullen or hostile;
without moral quality;
marked by misfortune;
based on the grotesque, morbid,
or unpleasant aspects of life;
illegal or underground;
         determine the designer of said delineation,
          deliberately false or intentionally misleading;
pertaining to any of the various populations characterized by **dark skin**
       dark-skin,
         dark skin—
                darkskin.

Regurgitate star-spangled banner, cough up countries tis(ing) of thee,
take several knees
at pledges of allegiance, vomit up purple mountains,
vote, vote at primaries, vote cause it's your right, vote to make change—
                Don't vote!
U.S. currency has the right idea,
         dead presidents—
the epitome of progress
spit up politics,
march in streets for soldiers lost,
             soldiers,
       brothers
babies,
          presidential hopefuls
that never signed up for this war,
your war,
              their war

the sirens versus coloreds war
the boy, you don't belong here war,
on soil they've learned to call their own,
we've learned to call our own.

Remember home,
                        not Queens
or **Brooklyn,**
                        or Barbados,
                                          but the motherland,
spit out   white   America.

Wipe mouth
                                          of
                                      of me
                                  of booze
                                of vulgarity,
                            of fried chicken
                        of black vernacular
                      of watermelon juices
                of nigguh want a Masters,
wanna be massa?
want to—**claim**
                    the pyramids
but misappropriate rationality of the second amendment
rather
    disassociate responsibility for the young men **shot** in the South Side of Chicago
                                          bing!
                                                          score a hundred for genocide,

for the niggers joining gangs, banging across the nation
 ding!
 score a thousand more for genocide,
for the brothers entrepreneuring that **powder**
 those **pills**
 that cook-up
 ping!
 score a million more for genocide,
for taking the bait, feeding into Mother Liberty's ideology of the superpredator,
jumpsuits and appellation as a digit—
 slavery for the win.

I am not as you see me, as they see me,
 as the world sees me,
as I see through
 ghetto-tinted,
 bottle-blurred
 boozed-up ebony vision,
it's backwards in the mirror
 T E O P
not drunk,
not angry black man,
not the product of two immigrants who fell in love,
 product of jungle bunnies making jungle love,
but the byproduct of a
 s   p   a   c   e   d   o   u   t
 love,
a beautiful 166 square miles of black love molded in a melting pot
 and I'm dying—
 dying,

                                                                    dying as
                    a dying   human
     dying from   being   a   p   a   r   t
                                                              unaccepted,
unloved,
            un**derestimated,**
                                                    just a negro.
I'm not as you see me, as they see me,
                                                    as the world sees me
because they can't,
                                        don't,
                        don't try to,
don't care to,
            don't wanna see me   without labels,
and I can't see myself through the **darkness,**
                                double vision or empty shot glasses,
I'm trying to etch out a place where I belong,
                                                        where we—
            belong and are wanted,
                                in **academia**
                                    in society
in literature,
                writing songs of myself but singing songs of each other
in the four hundred and fifty-one degrees of Fahrenheit at which a book burns,
throughout the flames I remain
                                    remain
            remain,
                                                            UNSEEN
                                                            UNSEEN
                                                              unseen

            but **heard**—

THAT THING OF OURS & X-FACTOR MEMORIES

My stomach is a house
where carcinogens and ammunition
breakdance and battle
to see who gets the win

by stopping my heart from
beating tables in the lunch
room where my daughter spits
rhymes like a young Lauren

Hill miseducated about the genes
that wade in the flow of her
Caribbean waters; she's unaware
I can hear her

from my death bed practicing
cast-iron lyrics in a mirror
where tamarind complexion glistens
under a sun created by a God

that whispers for my return.
I'll miss these moments she
never knew existed more than
the conversations she'll hang onto.

SHAWN CARTER CORRECTIONAL FACILITY: INMATE A112266

Cancer is a word, not a sentence. —John Diamond

Fatigue is a seven-foot, one-inch, 422-pound dude
with gang tats sitting on my chest preventing diaphragm's expansion.
So if cancer is not a sentence
                                      then why the association with barrs?
Why is there an orange jumpsuit lodged onto the casing of brain-
       waves crashing with static and loss of signal
like cancer's on DVR and remission pauses—as if
there's a comma after each check-up I avoid at the infirmary
       until a cough forces me
to check crimson-tinged sputum smeared against the cobblestone,
       as if prison walkways are the coliseum block
now the gladiator inside is tired.
What more can I say?
Like midnight in Marcy Projects during a blackout,
       only teeth and sclera are visible but I'm still on lockdown.
This is how the shadow of solitary swallows me at random times of the day
       while others pretend to be free
               hooping and lifting weights in the yard.
Pimples and boils under the skin are mistaken for lumps
and just a few of my *99 problems*
                           now every shower is the equivalent of a new *threat*.
Fists, pounding walls, tiles
               cracking, soap dropping,
and the only reason I'm not dodging shivs
       is because my body is always the host of the weapon.
What *if I should die* and my wife has to watch me *fade to black* through a visitor's glass?
Stolen of my identity and renamed
like indigenous descendants arriving through Ellis Island from Bridgetown port
       or like the Kush travelling vast oceans as cargo
rechristened with slave names before words and numbers were embossed upon us—

Inmate A112266
                    a cancer ID.
Avoid all visitors, all telephone calls and all outside
           noise, it's the *encore* of thought inside
               cells growing.
No more conversations with my daughters or chronicles of the corner
           just *song cry*.
Riot gear can't protect the vulnerability left by confinement
family feuds are resolved, and friends don't comprehend the seclusion
           of an intrinsic 6 by 8
so loneliness is the only inmate who understands
           and my psychoanalyst is claustrophobic.
In the nothingness of the hole,
           my psychiatrist watches with an unrecognizable gaze of self-pity staring
at a hairless version of myself and I speak less.
Dry mouth is a preventative measure as not to gulp the mixture
           of Hudson from the shores of Sing Sing and the East River off Rikers Island
         slightly blended and seeping down my esophagus
as my 422 lb. cellmate, the *American gangster*, eases upward towards my throat.
Lying on a cot I regress from convict to baby in the arms of Doris Murray.
These *blueprint* memories of Gran-Gran remind me of
           the warden, a sixty-four-year old Indian woman who prays to
Shiva
           but insists a neon green-beam
will grant me parole in this *empire state of mind*,
will grant me something about serenity, accepting
           a sentence or knowing the difference

between house nigguh and field nigguh—lethargic mastication of meals with expectations
      of making out with aluminum toilets
      doubles the impact of weight loss
      as decay is mental——still nigger.
I scratch another line into the wall representing another day surviving lockdown
remembering that
                cancer was once a language everyone spoke in my living room,
and I fall to the cold concrete floor of a death row ward,
now the slam of cell-door eyelids forces the quiet to blanket me
      and sheep are counted in the fields where stem cells are harvested and metastasize
      but never for me,
my *hard knock life* displays dreams overflowing with shrapnel and quick deaths
      until morning—roll-call.

In the midst of full-stream urination it happens, like a slap interrupting a conversation. Eight seconds of nothingness, and then it continues—the stream at the precipice of all my concerns.

I HAD A CONVERSATION WITH MY DAUGHTERS

My baby girl asks if I am gonna lose my hair?
I break eye contact and begin sweeping.
Her eldest sister hits her upside her head and says, "Too many questions."
In my living room, cancer is a language everyone speaks,

I break eye contact and begin sweeping.
Even writers have difficulty speaking though
in my living room cancer is a language everyone speaks.
Sometimes fatal thoughts disrupt the dialect.

Writers have difficulty speaking even though
we use words for damage control.
Fatal thoughts sometimes disrupt the dialect,
and to be honest, dialogue is driven by denial.

We spin words for a false sense of damage control
to alleviate vertigo from logic's carousel,
but to be honest, most dialogue is driven by denial.
The truth, like cancer, spreads viscerally

and alleviates vertigo from logic's carousel.
A worried smile is shared as we're lost in uncertainty,
and the truth is fast like cancer spreading viscerally.
I tuck fatigue and weakness behind my dimple

and we're lost in uncertainty sharing a worried smile
until my middle daughter slips through the door.
With fatigue and weakness already tucked behind a dimple,
she asks why we look like someone's dying?

As my middle daughter slips past the door,
she asks, "Why y'all look like someone's dying?"
and my baby girl asks, "Will you lose your hair?"
Her eldest sister hits her upside her head.
"Y'all ask too many questions!"

No one took it worst than my mother. She screamed. How I couldn't in the shower, or during the biopsy. She screamed for her, for me. I'm not Uncle Casper, Mummy. Medicine has come such a far way since the 80s; shit, so have music and literature. My brother storms out of the room as if it were contagious. Grabs his laptop. My father lies there. It wasn't a rum stupor or him waiting for the final bowl of a cricket match, it was the motionlessness associated with nucleo-genocide. His boy could possibly die before he could. His heart shut off for a second. There's nothing to say, nothing to do, and before the echo of the information could register, my mother's shrieks, of reliving her brother's death, seeped into his nasal cavity like smelling salts. My brother's looking up chemotherapy, radiation therapy, and all therapies that drain one's life in order to save it. "That's the shit dude from Spartacus just died from, ain't it." Yeah, Andy Whitfield. He and Uncle Casper. Score two for Hodgkins.

A BLACK FATHER'S FINAL DAYS OF STAGE IV TERMINAL THOUGHT-CANCER

canto i.

A poet uses the word apoptosis.
The dictionary says *triggered*; death of cells,
I read
        machine guns and metastatic prostate cancer
I say out loud
        bullet-hole hoodies and Hodgkin's lymphoma
I whisper
        it's ten o'clock and I do know where my children are:
        counting the bullets, the shell casings, the fragments of cloth
        intermingled with charred black flesh, traces of who they sat next to
        in 5th grade math, a cute boy's memory downgraded to a closed casket.

A friend's great-grand-someone named Don used to steal coal and ran before the cops closed in;
I read
        the don had cold steel and stole black kids
I said out loud
        the officer donned a standard police firearm
        and stole a child's life...shot in the torso...left in the cold.
A frozen park at the Cudell Recreation Center in Cleveland, Ohio, tells the story
but my mind
        was thinking about the cold steel machines of my daughter's first mammogram.

canto ii.

In Valley Stream, New York,
close to Green Acres Mall,
a seventeen-year-old girl is called into a room

where each breast is compressed horizontally,
then diagonally between two plastic plates to be
man-handled and squished
for pics that won't be posted on her social media sites,
all because of her father's blood.
#Origin

In Beavercreek, Ohio, there's a faded chalk outline
of a twenty-two-year-old black male in a Walmart
across from the Mall at Fairfield Commons
with a department store at the end
though other stores are entirely gone.
No more candy store or photo studio, the Express is closed as well as the Banana Republic.
Two plastic-framed, metal-plated signs remain with the words *final days*,
everything else is empty—like the contents of clips attached to the semi-autos aimed
at unarmed black men
with futures similar to that mall.
#Conclusion

canto iii.

I'm spitting words, clots that form the end of remission.
Around my wrist,
	a white hospital band screams patient,
vision blurry, I think I see the missing name
	in bluish blots of script
	an inked, curved messy script, but it's not my name.
Around my neck,
	an arm that serves, a nightstick that protects—

grant her the serenity God to know
        the difference between those
who arrive when my child dials 9-1-1,
        the protectors or the devilishly acquitted
who always escape
        from justice.

Around the corner,
        there's a gun store next to a pharmacy
with people standing outside of each one puffing cancer sticks.
        Death is sold at both locations and a sticker in the drugstore window reads:
Medical marijuana to deal with the prior, sold here too. It makes no sense.
        I'm at a bus stop watching
the butchers on the beat preying on the hustlers,
        the hustlers aware of five-O but preying
on clueless high schoolers
        in rival school-colored hoodies,
when they shout *Gang! Gang! Gang!* they really just mean their friends.
        I'm dialing my middle daughter and listening to a ring-back tone
        of Craig Mack's *Flavor in Your Ear*, the remix,
        she was hooked the first time I played it.
        Sirens zip down the block as she answers,
the call drops.
        I never hear her voice. Nothing makes sense.
Around the depot
        everyone has a destination:
        Harlem, Bridgetown, Toronto, Queens, London, Accra.
There's no escaping leukemia and buses don't have wings.

canto iv.

I'm in a dilapidated room watching paint chips leap from the ceiling.
The sun shreds through venetian blinds and slithers past sheetrock
      into the radiation center as spring disembarks
where Brooklyn is Belgrade
      and these beams rearrange my thoughts.
Building a wall won't help when there's a knock at the door. It's not the Potter.
Cancer is here.
There's nowhere for us to hide—we'll be living in cancer,
dwelling in cancer, eating in cancer, breathing in
      cancer that will consume us,
even if we temporarily get away there's no avoiding cancer,
      it's a whole 'nother animal.

Somewhere one by one
collective beasts roam
the plural, the two
not the ram and the bull
      but the cancer and the bullet— precious metals
gold, copper, and iron
no one mentions lead
      strung around their necks like collars
no one mentions shards
      stuck in alveoli collapsing lung
no one mentions their necks
      shrunk by Miranda rights wronged. Threats and derogatory terms
          whispered in tar baby ear,
no one mentions injustice is rape while a badge
      penetrates our mind and imprints revulsion,
no one mentions revolution is a recurring funeral.

canto v.

They see us as cancer.
A group of idle, substandard tumors of ethnic origin; a socially disenfranchised
batch of shooting range targets,
melanin bullseye on skull; not royalty but peasants stricken with a magnetic melanoma;
watch how we attract bullets and bleed poison.
Our offspring are glitches in the matrix;
      Neo doesn't exist.
None of us can dodge or stop death pellets.

They see me as cancer,
a single dark thing like a virus packing blackness into a gunnysack.
Murkiness tucked under a hoodie.
Watch up close, magical dark-skinned errors at the edge of the Hudson
skimming the poverty line sketched by the one-percenters—blue lives conjoined with all lives,
      it's a competition of mattering.
And the apex is a clenched black fist off Murdock
      where dime-bags of sonic boom flood Chinese restaurants and corner stores
      then becomes a refurbished Nostrand
where opioids are wrapped in receipts at Starbucks and Chipotles,
the transitioning of my old neighborhoods makes me forget about my youngest daughter
      witnessing the world written in bold ugliness.

canto vi.

I can't make out her face.
I call her over to me from across a street of cobblestone and corrupt cells,
      but she can't hear me,
I can barely hear myself between the rat-a-tat tatter of the machine gun
and the mothers bawling as their wooden-box babies are being lowered into forever.
An elevator dings in the background and my heart races like a ?uestlove drum solo.
I'm freezing. I try to move, but my beaten and bruised body
doesn't respond. I explode—
        My blanket is shredded,
and shrapnel and ball bearings are embedded into the mattress beneath me.
        I try to move, but movement is a teenager whose nervous
    hands can't stand still
        when an officer screams freeze,
I implode.

I can't make out my body.
My left hand, handcuffed to a stop sign in front of a bodega,
my right hooked up to an adriamycin drip.
        No recollection of transport;
My legs in a fixed position as radiation beams scorch everything in a straight line.
My abdomen is bloated and swollen
      from the kicks and nightstick signatures of the 105th precinct.
The nurse has a taser.
An officer with a clipboard asks if I want something for the pain.
I can't make out his words
     everything is confusion as hearing ceases and little black girls cry
     then call out for Daddy.

I stop and revisit my ancestors, my bloodline, my lineage, and broughtupsy, for they are the ones who have sparked this, coming of age realization of identity in this work. I thought of the "mothers and grandmothers who died with their real gifts stifled within them" that Walker speaks of, possibly Gran-Gran. I imagine voices of the dead, and the millions of tar-babies buried in their mother's wombs with creativity, the poets that bled out from open wounds courtesy of the lash; eyes bulging of the essayists that were lynched in the South for reading and writing; the compliant novelists shot dead because they fit the description; the stage 4 short story writers whose frail bodies couldn't handle the chemotherapy; the playwrights who never got treatment and decided to smoke in lieu of diagnosis and prognosis; silenced laureates that have been reduced to hashtags and memories; their voices and what it sounds like in variation to my opportunity.

THE TAIL END OF RISING

My wife tells me we should go watch the fall foliage but

I'm kneeling on asphalt watching these white lies
Sam Cooke describes in lyrics like *change*,
               leaves fall.
This foliage ain't recognizable cause
               leafs—drop.
These trees don't grasp 'em like our predecessors.
They dangled; anatomies of charcoal complexion be earrings.
Our soul be jewels.
Our spirits be diamonds glimmering back to the essence
      as life leaves us.
Whimsical whispers on the coattails of the wind
       we kneel with ashy dark knees on concrete
       watching the facade because colors seem to shift
from tints of green to red, maybe orange or a yellow
to brown but everything still screams
                   Whites only.

Autumn feels like *"Get on the ground nigger!"*

The fragility of a trachea, crushed
such that
we can't breathe in this frigid oxygen.
It's excessively caucasian,
too toxic, its carcinogenic characteristics thicken it.
It's corn starch.
                   It's cinnamon stuck in our throat
coating salivary glands, and since we
can't swallow the truths of hated pigmentation

melanin chokes.
                        We fall now, rather than hang—
is this the change Sam sang about?
Evergreens and oaks which spoke novels of our last rites are now barren,
bare branches hover over bullet-ridden bodies of obsidian,
Hip-Hop don't echo like negro spirituals did when the leaves of grass spoke,

Can you hear them sing songs?

Our daughters once played in piles of a tree's tears after we
        shoveled them.
Angels making angels
and as the hues of October dawn
they become mothers.
Mothers scared to let their children play in the grass, let alone in
        the leafs that leave us.

See our trauma be autumn,

be the things that fall from our withering arms.
Our historical biographies be cranberry sauce covered sweaters
        two weeks before thanksgiving,
be crimson-stained pavement——there's no replacing the mantles
        of slave ships,
and pellets from pistols don't rustle through midnight.
They are like hurricanes,
loud outcries that shatter both bone and bark,
creating fissures in our future's family tree of existence.

Our sons once climbed the accessory of ancestral murder.
Once reached for sun and clouds before mic and ball,
but the sun burned our flesh as the clouds laughed.
Then bales of cotton turned to
baskets of leaves turned to
mischievous acts as semi-automatic leaf blowers were handed out
      in neighborhoods where trees don't grow
and branches don't tell tales of togetherness like our elders.
The only goal is to rake in the proverbial doe, so
our landscape is forever stained with a
              skewed portrait.

My wife is constantly telling me to come take in the foliage
      but I remind her
of the tail end of rising,
all we do is fall——

BONUS TRACKS

A CONVERSATION I HAD WITH MY DAUGHTER

who says people with cancer
have a higher survival rate

than young black men in America
because there are substantial services

that may prolong the quality of life,
reduce pain, and kill cancer cells

should the unfortunate be fortunate
enough to be diagnosed early,

whereas when you're born
a black male it's already too late.

BLOOD CHANGES AND BEST FRIENDS BECOME STRANGERS

My blood is always fighting now:
racism swimming in plasma drowning in the shadows
       of delusion my brain swears is *power to the people* blackness;
white blood cells kick the shit outta red blood cells. See they are the boxers
       getting in the ring with disease and battling bacteria for dozens of rounds,
right jab!
       without trainers whispering subtleties and words of encouragement,
left jab!
       without nurturing bruises and never blocking,
it's haymaker after haymaker in between uppercuts and hooks, the defenders.

Red blood cells take the plummeting but never surrender
       cause *we real cool*,
holding oxygen in deep like weed smoke while
       sneaking out starlets of carbon dioxide.
Never out for the count,
       they outlast the whites, absorb blows
       in black-lives-matter melanin and intimidate platelets.

The bouts become emotional around the heart,
       many stop fighting and relax,
let music fill 'em up and pump
                       to a beat sliding through valves and getting sucked into tear ducts,
       they quit the fight,
many cluster up and rap Matisyahu at Hip-Hop peace summits,
                       but at the brain
they get serious and yell proper names at one another,
You stubborn erythrocytes! or the popular *oh to the rectum with you, leukocyte scum!*

Once upon a time they co-existed like ah DJ and an emcee,
        functioned as a team streaming through anatomy
organs yelling in harmony for
        R-B-Cs and W-B-Cs!
They keep the body oxygenated and fight off infection in a non-coagulated unison
        and then slap high-fives and beat box off the walls of the lungs
while rhymes echo through auditory canals.
        Are blood cells in the houuuusssseee!
Red blood cells are responsible for pigmentation,
        gang affiliation accusations, Nigerian-tone and sun-bathing,
Metallica-type fragments found in skulls of teenagers across America
        with no answers towards the conception of repugnance—but

white blood cells are responsible for turning on themselves
with an eagerness to fight, they're cramped up—bar brawling in lungs,
        in stomachs, in pancreas, in prostate, in brain, in lymph nodes,
metastasizing and spreading; the only relief each round is 5-FU.
My blood is always fighting,
                      one part blaming the other part and vice
        versa,
my complete blood count is a session of finger pointing in a test tube,
        evaluating the brain's distress with unknown measures and
            wrapping knuckles avoiding knockouts.

THE HOST LEAVES

once becoming a patient, and the cancer remains.

I think about my limits and question if I'm doing these spirits that have died for us, and in vain, any justice. Am I disturbing the souls of those stolen from us ahead of their time? Are my words paying homage and bringing awareness to the senseless taking of their lives in the comparison of cancer of the body and a cancerous mentality in an authoritative way that does justice to black literature? With every page I think about black expressionism and how it identifies me. I'm refocusing on word choice. I think of the word victim, the word target, the word patient, the word abnormal, and how each of them equates to America, how they strip us, strip me of identity; also, how every word I write and revise gains a little bit of who I am back. Nothing can control a writer unless that writer allows him or herself to be controlled. This is my way of strong-arming my trauma, as the cliché goes, facing my fears; head on, with a pen, praying that when I'm uncertain my ancestors grab my hand and continue the process of ink formulating these ideas. Let their remembrance be eternalized in marriage to the immortality of my humble thought.

There is so much freedom in flying, cutting through the air at uncanny speeds...like a bullet, a projectile or other shot fired from a gun which has zero business playing pinball inside the bodies of young black men or women, ricocheting off organs as white police officers attain high scores and paid leave.

THERE'S MANURE IN THE MEDIA'S WHEELBARROW

when black bodies
are furnished with

bluecoat munitions
and left in the street

for interpretation,
so much depends

upon how the story
breaks.

CHAOS ON CANFIELD DRIVE: TIMELINE FOR A BODY

Timeline for a Body: 4 Hours in the Middle of the Street
New York Times • Aug. 23, 2014

                              after
Brown   shot   police
        remained
              horrified.   Brown
                                    children
                        recorded

    Brown
body   ultimately   shooting
           officials.
Brown   would become
worldwide
                   and   America
ask,   why
     help   the outrage?   disrespect
                    the message
            in broad daylight

f   Brown   death!   view   and   review
                        police control

                      homicide—   call

        It
  chaos   where
Brown   step   inside,
                  Gunshots
   work

                                      right away.

                    A white sheet   seen
was no
surprise
        in   Brooklyn.
                                    Brown
                                     time
                                        usually difficult,
        Brown   voice

                    dead—shot

                                        a   larger force,
                                                    by
                                                        bystanders
In   close   distance,

            a paramedic   a pulse
                            a sheet

a family friend,   a   teenager
    or   nothing.
            Nobody came.   nobody   said   sorry.   Nobody said nothing.
                            Brown
                                     body
                                            yell   and

                            grabbed
                                                        A cop
he   said.

99

                        he hung
                                    for more than two hours

exposed   in
                 New York City,   said
the temperature
                              declined
              while   Brown body
                         struggle...   and
                           shell casings detect
the   little   body,
he said.
                something like   tension
grew.   they   said.
         "homicide   not   control."
  another   Brown   body,
              a blue
                     sport.
Michael Brown's body was checked into the morgue at 4:37 p.m., more than four
and a half hours after he was shot.

100

I rummaged through libraries, documentaries, and medical magazines for evidence verifying the magnetism of melanin. I found no proof that it exists, some may say like racism.

THE ILLSTREET BLUES OF SHEEP'S CLOTHING

The wolf thought to himself what a tender young creature, what a nice plump mouthful.
—The Brothers Grimm, 1812

Wolves shouldn't wear badges since they prey on unarmed animals
    that don't resemble them.
Animals who howl to a moon that will never accept tar-baby skin-tone

like mine which gathers in Adventist churches, praying these cannibals atone
    for cancerous sins of the core being,
praying my daughters' voices are compliant and their hands more visible than their darkness.

A dark perceived as a threat in red riding hoodie.
    A blackness that apparently leaps off our skeleton and surrounds wolves,
interfering with privileged air and infesting the right to bear arms of animosity.

Nigrescence that shrieks in the woods like hangman knots.
Nigritude silenced by rusty blades castrating the indigenous.

During the *quiet storm*, wolves patrol with teeth better to eat dark meat with,
    piercing sable bodies like projectiles from glock-9s,
bites that tear through ebony flesh and reload.

What big ears they have listening to the screams of onyx mothers cradling limp bodies
    that tried to stay on the path as forewarned,
heavier now because of forced lead intake.

Caliginous bodies that don't resemble the precious animal that merely
    went for a stroll to see Granny.
Nebulous bodies with arms bent behind back like chicken wings

deep fried in viciousness as skin glistens to huge eyes
      better for wolves to see victims as perps
looking down the barrel of a penumbra,

before hearing the deep howl, before a bellow better to greet black sheep with,
before huffing and puffing, these wolves focus only on
      blowing the house down.

Woodcutters and lumberjacks are mythical creatures.
Houses of straw, stick, nor brick
      could prevent the clamor of wolves in sheep's clothing.

There's no hiding at Gran-Gran's house
if one should make it past the big bad wolves
      breakdancing to the sirens and the outcry of steel.

WHAT IF ERIC GARNER WAS CHOKED OUT BY THROAT CANCER

his trachea crushed
by metastasis of his jugular node causing him to have trouble
      swallowing, his voice changed as he mumbled the terrifying words
"I can't breathe"—11 times
which audio picks up after the first one,
it sounds clear and concise in videos with police officers speaking
      and background noises don't distort,
eleven times
      and those behind the blue wall of silence were trying to save him,
          were trying CPR,
trying the Heimlich, trying to work against: obesity; hypertensive cardiovascular disease;
      acute and chronic bronchial asthma;
the color of skin that apparently looks stunning in a pair of fancy platinum handcuffs;
the cause—the loosies he smoked, not *presumably* sold
decompressed neck of carcinoma chokeholds
for 15 to 19 seconds
      from fifteen to nineteen seconds
      surrendering his
6'3", 350lb. frame,
his six-foot-three-inch, three-hundred-and-fifty-pound frame
      limp and unconscious...
I can't breathe
          thinking what if this was one of my daughters,
fifteen to nineteen years old
      and being attacked—
Thank God Garner was turned on his side for 7 minutes
for seven whole minutes
      without checking his thready pulse; without giving him oxygen;
without giving him room to breathe because

a cuffed and subdued fallen giant needs four officers
········and a knee on his head; this would probably clear my airway—
seven whole minutes
········without compressions because his heart couldn't deal with
········the strangulation cancer was causing,
a cancer with zero indictments.

I have an oncologist for my fear of recurrence, who do I see for my fear of being killed over the color of my skin? Because my psychiatrist is a reflection of myself with thoughts darker than my tone and a tone as vicious as the hunters. He sits in mirrors watching me, mouthing Baldwin, "To be a Negro in this country and to be relatively conscious is to be in a rage almost all the time"; and though I may not be your Negro, we lock eyes as he whispers to me *I'm the nigguh they gon' get!*

WHEN THE RAGE TAKES OVER

Yesterday I wrote ah poem.
Yesterday I wrote ah poem about the revolution.
Yesterday I wrote ah poem about the revolution being televised and I
        wasn't around to watch it because 12 hours before I killed two
                cops.
Yesterday I wrote ah poem about the revolution that wouldn't be
        televised because all they showed
was the cop's bodies dangling from ah single red oak;
the noose created by multiple garbage bags,
his hands
pinned up in ah don't-shoot formation his
uniform graffiti'd with the words breathing is overrated, him I caught jogging
        in ah no cop zone,
another cop behind him holding him in ah chokehold, all of their knees
        torn off,
all lives matter carved into their white flesh,
every spin their bodies make
        skittles fall from mouth, from pocket, from where their dicks
used to be these
        human piñatas.

Today I wrote ah poem.
Today I wrote ah poem about the revolution.
Today I wrote ah poem about the revolution being televised and I
        wasn't around to watch it because 24 hours ago I killed two
                more cops.
Today I wrote ah poem about the revolution that wouldn't be
        televised because all they showed
was them in the squad car riddled with 50 bullets
and the CDs they confiscated with music by RUN,

no DMC just Run nigger and we'll still shoot you in your back,
ah trunk full of loosies
       that cause cancer but not the same cancer provided by badges, these animals,
one with his wallet loaded and cocked,
41 shots in him while the other was cuffed with an air gun in his lap probably ready to aim
       at some young punk on ah park bench,
these are the benchmarks of history.

Tomorrow I'll write ah poem.
Tomorrow I'll write ah poem about the revolution.
Tomorrow I'll write ah poem about the revolution being televised but I
       won't be around to watch it because by then 36 hours would
         have passed since I killed the last
            three cops.
Tomorrow I'll write ah poem about the revolution that won't be
       televised because all they'll show
is the house where these cops lived together on some
       three's company shit,
one in his own backyard cuffed and face down, ah single shot to his back, like strange Fruitvale
stationed only ah short distance from where he
       crashed his car,
two women inside, one on the couch holding a nickel-plated iPhone in
       one hand in which
the game she played had familiar sounds of gun fire, and ah three
       musketeers chocolate bar in the other,
whose diabetic value is lethal to blacks,
I felt threatened...
the last one lying in her bed, dreaming...
dreaming of ah way to end racism in America,

dreaming of quitting this corrupt blue shield and start fresh as
        something incorruptible like ah politician;
she bled out before she could wake or scream.

As I type this,
tears stream down my face because
I never got to say goodbye to you,
I never got to tell you I've never fallen in love faster,
I never got to kiss anyone goodbye,
but the sirens are blaring behind me and all I can do is press send,
before I do I'll sign it,
your blac k kinnhggbb
        nbbbfnj
              cjcjdwb
                      wbnmmmjuygvfb

"The revolution won't be televised but we will stylize every breath we take back from the ones they stole, and air they a$$ out repeatedly; in syndication…on every network."
@wyze78

STEREOTYPES & THE N-WORD CONTROVERSY

"For the face that the jakes pinned as being a nigger
So he gives him everything that he thinks a nigger should take,
And you ask him how to spell it, and he responds please make up your mind,
You niggaz is either niggers or you ain't."
—Skyzoo, "Everybody's Fine"

Everybody is not fine where black and brown faces collide with blue wall,
where mesothelioma and bullet fragments become common cause of death
    so headlines become bylines and crime converts to common courtesy;

where a casket is seen as the release from hard living,
where latchkey kids don't fear being Macaulay Culkin'ed,
    home alone often so home is an orphanage

where brothers and sisters are covered in cyber scars and blisters, and suicide is teenage lotto,
their daddies are in the country's racist work program rocking jumpsuits
    the color of forty-five's face,
so Mama spends Sundays Kaepernicking in the tabernacle expecting the Lord
    we've been waiting on, since wading in the river to deliver more than
    EBTs and ramen noodles this month,

somewhere roaches and mice are living good without heat in the teflon-coated winter
    of Far Rockaway or Freeport or Ferguson or Flint,
where lights are flickering, and purchased prize possessions are all that we possess,
where bellies are not sucked in and no one is drinking flat tummy tea,
    ribcages are protruding from emptiness,

where joints are rolled in toilet tissue
and every argument ends in gun-brandishing hypocritical bloodshed
and is intensified by brown liquor
and starts with Talib Kweli over a Hi-Tek beat syncing the streets and

a stereotype reality on day one, minute one:
of the training with Mahoney and Hightower, but beat into their logic
by professors, by teachers, by parents, by presidents, by forefathers, by
    the forefathers of the 2.3 billion acres of land stolen, raped on,
    murdered for, enslaved over, flown into, and returned on the
    starred and striped silver platter in plain sight—
socialized, *accepted*, and widespread,
    so historians and bystanders take visual biopsies and both become
    oncologists...
yet everybody's fine—

I heard the term cellular suicide and froze. Body became numb, like it was then, on that metal slab. I couldn't feel my feet; everything from the tingling in my thigh to the concrete was motionless. Days after, I still couldn't write these thoughts down. The pen became larger than my hands—it metastasized. Seriously, pens grow in the midst of misunderstanding. I couldn't comprehend how my hands copycatted the actions of my feet; they too couldn't move, I was stuck. It wasn't weed or whiskey; it was my brain contemplating how to infiltrate these cells that have seemed to hijack a part of my anatomy. I wasn't going to be killed from the inside. Nucleo-genocide.

ADULTS DON'T LIE AWAKE THINKING ABOUT MONSTERS

night lights don't help as brain matter differentiates
lump and fissure:
the first forces fingers to run over surface with
unexplainable extension from self, from
charcoal speed bump of skin signaling the reduced white blood cells to pump

brakes as caution flags now come in chemo pills; as the other stands,
black aperture—fingers become tampons and plug holes, though dreams
of daughters jumping brooms still escape body in puddles of plasma.
the mind never thinks to ask the hands how death feels,
the texture of moisture-less flesh after a sunbeam bears down daily, or

the singed chasm a projectile concocts when
it tears through epithelial layers, knowing the body is sixty percent water and
feeling it flow pass fingers like a faucet.
the brain, incessant on fatality runs laps at Roy Wilkins Park,
pondering *pun* Lonsurf and gloves needed to hold pills,

now death is in the midst of the palm like melanin in a red blood cell,
the cause of the remarkable is the same reason
amazing grace is sung in sullen tombstone acapellas.
these are the boogeymen in the closets of survivors,
under the bed but wrapped in king-size covers.

adults lay wake engineering hollow-point hunting
and themselves as game,
deep penetration of metallic fragments and organ lodging,
the entry site, no exit wounds
because being shot is as septic to the mind as malignancy.

adults would rather *duppies* come from cemeteries,
or zombies breathing down lump-less neck or
touching non-targeted body, unfortunately
the big C is a manic cyclops navigating within the bloodstream
and black magic has survived monsters for too many centuries
      to bother losing sleep now.

THE ART OF RECURRENCE

The refrigerator door opens: orange juice, spinach, broccoli, kale, massive amounts of bottled water, ginger ale, ginger beer, lemons, cucumbers, tofu, lettuce, cabbage, the lists of vegetables could actually go on and on, but no, it's unnecessary. We walk into the bathroom and open the medicine cabinet and there are six bottles of vitamin C, amino acids, wellness formula pills, probiotics, then your regular medicine for headaches, stomachaches, antacids, and such. We leave and head towards the kitchen to open the cupboard, only to realize one of the kids left it open as usual. I should just take the door off the hinges, we chuckle. I swing it open a little further to check the contents: tumeric, garlic, dandelion root tea, green tea, ginger tea, ginger, ginger snaps, ginger cuts, yep. Ginger is the West Indian panacea. *Remember back in 1991 when we fell off the bike and scraped our knee on those damn rose bushes.* Oh yeah, and I came in the house bawling! Daddy threw a plastic cup at me, told me something bout *"You mekking too much noise"* and how he couldn't hear Pat Sajak. Gran-Gran took a piece of ginger and a grater, rinsed my knee with water, then a splash of white rum, and then grated ginger and pressed against that open wound. Yep, I screamed even louder. Damn ginger!

Every April, when it's time for our yearly physical, we cringe. Cringe knowing that the contacts part of the phone is packed with doctors who love poking and prodding. All types of 'ists': cardiologist, podiatrist, radiologist, hematologist, oncologist. Proctolo—not yet. This might be the reason why the primary care physician doesn't get on our damn nerves. Google how much more do doctors make when they run a hundred tests as opposed to fifty. We chuckle. *"Receptionist—I need to make an appointment."*

We keep water by the bedside. Hearing a voice telling us to hydrate—in case we arise in the middle of the night choking, coughing, or spitting up blood. Yep. That's happened before but only once and I'm pretty sure we probably, definitely, might have just broken a blood vessel. That's it. Nothing outrageous. We keep a window open all year round, rather cracked in the winter months because we can't allow freezing air in or too many germs. Matter of fact cracked in the spring as well because pollen can be a prick and I'm not sure there's antihistamines in the medicine cabinet. We make sure to flip the mattress every month, so nothing gets too worn and even now with this hybrid of coils and memory foam we still spin it. Comfort over everything and whenever we wake up in the foreday morning we double check that sleep has been longer than three hours. Over three hours we're safe, anything less and it's nighttime, anxiety takes its mark on an Olympic size track. We neighborhood watch our body for night sweats and flank pain because Web MD says they're the early symptoms. We're awake.

Bathroom time. Urinate in a steady stream, not broken up please. Thank you. We shower with a disgusting precision. *Size matters* is what women say, we chuckle. Two hundred and sixty pounds, yes size matters but it's not about that. We rinse every inch. Soap up every inch. Wash off every inch. Examine—every—inch. Soap up again, wash off again. Deep tissue massage the soap into the flesh this second time and wash off with a tender vigorous rub. Dirt doesn't stand a chance. We pay close attention to the groin, right and left inguinal sections. Under the arms, the neck, the chest tissue. Everywhere there's nodes. We towel dry with taps and rubs, gently but very attentive. With some moisture still on the flesh we oil up with coconut oil, working in it yet still investigating. Any muscles extra sore from a workout past three days we use a roller to work out the kinks.

I think about Gran-Gran every time I smell coconut oil. I wish she was still with us, but I don't want her to come back. I have an issue with the term 'come back,' 'coming back,' and 'returned.' We've been going through the photo albums a lot recently, sometimes I think too much like I'm conjuring up a reunion and—yep! Too much thinking, maybe I should set up an appointment with a neurologist. We chuckle.

Spring means it's check-up time. Time for new examinations. Same old hospitals and diagnostic centers but a batch of new nurses. It seems like there's always someone awaiting my return. The thought of returning brings everything to a head again. The fridge. The medicine cabinet. The cupboard. All loaded with things that are supposed to fight cancer, keep the body healthy, keep the mind strong. Eliminate stomach cancer, pancreatic cancer, liver cancer. *What about the bottle of No. 7*. Shh! The doctors and reliving the tests. Pet scan. CT scan. Blood work. How's the numbers, you know how the numbers are. White blood cell count, still low. Still abnormal.

The bed. Make sure there's no flank pain. The windows. Make sure there no night sweats. The water to stay hydrated. The spitting up blood, that's because it's coming back as lung cancer, throat cancer. No it's not. The over excessive molesting myself in the shower checking every nook and cranny and hoping all lymph nodes are the size they should be, size matters! Praying that the flow of urine is solid and straight because it's coming back as prostate cancer. No it's not. We make sure we don't smoke and stay away from smokers to prevent it from coming back as lung cancer. I can't stand to think about it coming back. That *cold* room. The metal. The beam. The radiation machine. The silence. And now, we live like this. A shell of who I used to be, now split in two. The patient with cancer, and the patient with cancer coming back.

ON YOUR MARK, GET SET

Firecrackers don't go off at 2AM
on a rainy foreday morning in the middle of brisk October,
nor are they followed by sirens
battle-rapping shrieks of grief
from the myth known as black fathers—non-transgendered dope boys
        of color who try out for the Olympics
as the dollar cab is a hundred meters away (and no longer a dollar)
                      an M-80 rings out
they high jump fences,
long jump fresh cement with hand prints of new love
        that won't last
and anniversary dates that belong on tombstones.
                A cherry bomb explodes.
They shot put their lungs through clouded ghetto air,
clogged with an infusion of vape kissing marijuana smoke
and only cough just before their last breath escapes them.
            Space blasters and whispering palms
wake up underage aunties and uncles in preparation
        to prep
handkerchiefs to catch the family floods that the levies of cornea
        can't handle.
Babies see reflections of their past lives in tear drops,
but when flesh tears
witnesses are hushed by the fissures left in black babies stolen
        by the resounding
"Freeze!" that usually sounds like
                      screaming spiders and echo bombs
sold in clips of sixteen
triggered by premeditated celebrations by the blue wall.

Firecrackers
        that enter shadowed bodies
                and explode in a confetti of melanin
                creating Jackson Pollack paintings of organs
                and graffiti on the pavement
are not firecrackers at all,
        they are the souls of our ancestors tallying up the arrival of
        another one,
        they are the expression of hatred squeezed with the perfect
        precision of pressure to expel a fate
decided upon when they witness the hoodie,
the security blanket for black teens in America because it hugs them
when the streets told their fathers not to
        oh that's soft
when the streets told them not to allow their mothers to
        oh you're a baby.
Firecrackers don't chase our babies—
        are not dark-seeking missiles of destruction trying to
        eradicate a race (of cells) that simply want to belong,
        that's a mind-state, a choice,
                        that's cancer.
        the gunshot
Go!

I HAVE CONVERSATIONS WITH MY DAUGHTERS

where Birdie sits on Gran-Gran's lap
teaching her about Tik Tok
and her chuckles are interrupted by two coughs
followed by bloodless spit slamming its way into more spit pooled
in a mint enamel mug
whose
purpose is no longer to carry coffee but to catch the puddles.

A conversation where Sheryl tells me the perils
of deep sleep,
overdosing on anesthesia this selective amnesia won't let me forget it. I reject sharing birthdays with
friends
cause good 'mourning' sounds the same when that birthday's shared
with a cousin who wouldn't wake up. Hospitals

are the basements and boiler rooms I swore
I saw Freddy Krueger in,
my childhood nightmares didn't
consist
of radiation and IVs and old men bonding in gowns
but arguing about which was more hot going down:
the chemo pills or the nurse.

We talk, my teenage daughters and I,
about their friends and antics, the blue wall addicts who
need no particular reason to shoot up— brown bodies
of
hope like heroin, I wonder if they felt like zombies

or heroes afterwards, both invincible.
This beautiful first kill that creates
puddles
of machine gun tears, the sounds of black
parents rat-ta-tat-tatting in the hours

in which they count their most zzz. I
remember every word,
every shrill as I fell at the mid-section of a casket
like
the organ keys struck star-spangled anger
I couldn't understand

why death knocked on doors
yet chest felt thumps vigorously. Trauma
is interwoven in the threads of
black
reality without Tyler Perry plays to further
perpetuate our—my

biggest fears. I explained to them that
cancer is so similar to police violence and
folk
don't understand how nervousness travels to the next location
of a body even when you're innocent, I mean healthy,
I mean you lie on that table with your hands up never knowing.

I had a conversation with my daughters and asked:
whose friends consist of puddles, like black folk?

I HAD A CONVERSATION WITH MY FATHER

about shoveling snow that he will never taste
      on the tip of his tongue again,
there's ah specific method he tells me *suh I won't catch backache*
      as if it were Cancer or Covid-19;
about currying chicken at 5 in the morning
      when my daughters are fast asleep
          dreaming—
different than Martin and Langston,
theirs more in sync with the audible sound of his voice,
the speed of his tone,
the inflection of happiness mixed with ah Bajan accent,
how pitch is ah concoction of heat and sweetness like Delish pepper sauce.

Emphasis is a spry eighty-year-old voice box
shaking like an '86 Chrysler Reliant K,
the one my mother drove for a hundred thousand miles 'til it was content
with everything it had provided and was ready
to go gentle into that good night,
where the ancestors await with open arms, calloused hands,
and strong backs.
BiPAP machine. Air flow. His 'ort, talk later' was stifled.

I understand now—
he didn't want to leave a messy corpse.
He wanted the reaper to visit him on his own turf, in bed
      with his wife of 49 years
where his loins could rise and fall
like a leaf we'd catch when strays shatter trees
or when branches snap cause the body's too heavy.
It should be leafs, not leaves...
      for not all black fathers do.

Confusion is ah pill in the bloodstream and depression
chased with fatigue is ah helluva cocktail on the rocks
    that one's lungs emulate
        three weeks into the virus.
He just wanted to be somewhere in between Barbados and what 30 years of labor blooms,
home.
I just wanted him to stay in that hospital,
the equivalent to the apartment he got me out of,
I was greedy.

I don't grow green with hope.
Too versed in conversations I despise,
my heart darkens, shrivels, and becomes angostura.
How can black people write about flowers at a time like this?
How can I celebrate my anniversary?
    knowing that as this conversation ends
      the only time I will hear him
      is as the wind deviates to whisper *shyte* in my ear
or when I burn my arm on that blahsted pot cuz I ain burn the curry long enough,
his chuckle, concealed behind my cuss words,
echoes fuh an instant just long enough fuh me to recognize.
Now, his laughter is merely the touch of the God he knew
    as a young black boy
pelting stones at the Caribbean Sea,
praying his children would release his ashes there.
Ventilator. Coma. He never said goodbye back.

I continue to smile, praying that Daddy is smiling along with me; I continue to write, in hopes that the byproduct of this work will urge a youth of color to pick up a pen and write the chronicles of his or her own diaspora, the struggles of his or her people in finding their identity, their fears and experiences breathing freedom to their soul, either on paper or over a beat, or on a stage, anywhere they can embrace the sensation of being abnormal; somewhere on Brandon Beach while a rooster crows at the break of dawn during fishing season, when the tide is low and children bathe in the sea water that slows the metastasis of cancer; before Mummy *hafi ti tek dem ti Sabbath school* and before finding out that one of their schoolmates who *leff home fuh ah bettah life in di states*, was gunned down on Farmers Blvd. by the same people who are paid to protect his liberties…and he utters words from Slick Rick's "La Di Da Di" to the *tick tock ya don't stop, to the tick tick ya don't quit, Hit it!* and continues scribing through the tears, through the smiles, despite the trauma.

ABOUT THE AUTHOR

Roger Wyze Smith is a Brooklyn-born poet of Bajan heritage, raised in Queens, NY. A working class, married father of three, Smith is the author of two self-published collections of poetry, *Laundromats & Lounges* (2013) and *Chambers of a Beating Heart* (2015). His third release *French Kissed Black Roses* (2015) won third place in the Local Gems NaPoWriMo chapbook contest. Smith was a 2012 Inspired Works Contest Winner, the 2017 Louis Armstrong House Archives Writer-in-Residence, and served as co-editor of poetry on *Armstrong Literary Online Magazine* 2018-2019. He holds a BA *cum laude* in English from Molloy College, an MFA in creative writing and literary translation from CUNY/Queens College, and is a member of Lambda Iota Tau Literary Honor Society.

NOTES:

The Audre Lorde quotes on pages 43 and 46 are from *Sister Outsider: Essays and Speeches* (Crossing Press, 1985).

Mávros Thánatos (page 60): The Black Death. The great epidemic of bubonic plague swept across Europe in the mid 14th century and killed between one-third to one-half of the population within months. It was carried by the fleas of black rats.

The Langston Huges quote (page 63) is from his 1926 essay "The Negro Artist and the Racial Mountain."

"Shawn Carter Correctional Facility: Inmate A112266" (page 70): "barr" refers to the Epstein-Barr virus. It is the cause of infectious mononucleosis, associated with various non-malignant, premalignant, and malignant lymphoproliferative diseases such as Hodgkin's lymphoma. The italicized phrases are references to the songs of Jay-Z, whose birth name was Shawn Carter.

ABOUT THE WORD WORKS

Since its founding in 1974, The Word Works has steadily published volumes of contemporary poetry and presented public programs. Its imprints include The Washington Prize, The Tenth Gate Prize, The Hilary Tham Capital Collection, and International Editions.

Monthly, The Word Works offers free programs in its Café Muse Literary Salon. Winners of the Jacklyn Potter Young Poets Competition are presented in the June Café Muse program. Other Word Works programs have included "In the Shadow of the Capitol," a symposium and archival project on the African American intellectual community in segregated Washington, D.C.; the Gunston Arts Center Poetry Series; the Poet Editor panel discussions at The Writer's Center; Master Class work-shops; and writing retreats in Tuscany, Italy.

As a 501(c)3 organization, The Word Works has received awards from the National Endowment for the Arts, the National Endowment for the Humanities, the D.C. Commission on the Arts & Humanities, the Witter Bynner Foundation, Poets & Writers, The Writer's Center, Bell Atlantic, the David G. Taft Foundation, and others, including many generous private patrons.

An archive of artistic and administrative materials in the Washington Writing Archive is housed in the George Washington University Gelman Library. The Word Works is a member of the Community of Literary Magazines and Presses and its books are distributed by Small Press Distribution.

wordworksbooks.org

OTHER WORD WORKS BOOKS

Annik Adey-Babinski, *Okay Cool No Smoking Love Pony*
Emily August, *The Punishments Must Be a School*
Jennifer Barber, *The Sliding Boat Our Bodies Made*
Rachel J. Bennett, *Mothers and Other Fairy Tales*
Karren L. Alenier, *Wandering on the Outside*
Andrea Carter Brown, *September 12*
Willa Carroll, *Nerve Chorus*
Grace Cavalieri, *Creature Comforts / The Long Game: Poems Selected & New*
Abby Chew, *A Bear Approaches from the Sky*
Nadia Colburn, *The High Shelf*
Henry Crawford, *The Binary Planet*
Barbara Goldberg, *Berta Broadfoot and Pepin the Short / Breaking & Entering: New and Selected Poems*
Akua Lezli Hope, *Them Gone*
Michael Klein, *The Early Minutes of Without*
Deborah Kuan, *Women on the Moon*
Frannie Lindsay, *If Mercy*
Elaine Magarrell, *The Madness of Chefs*
Chloe Martinez, *Ten Thousand Selves*
Marilyn McCabe, *Glass Factory*
JoAnne McFarland, *Identifying the Body*
Leslie McGrath, *Feminists Are Passing from Our Lives*
Kevin McLellan, *Ornitheology*
A. Molotkov, *Future Symptoms*
Ann Pelletier, *Letter That Never*
W.T. Pfefferle, *My Coolest Shirt*
Ayaz Pirani, *Happy You Are Here*
Robert Sargent, *Aspects of a Southern Story / A Woman from Memphis*
Julia Story, *Spinster for Hire*
Barbara Ungar, *After Naming the Animals*
Julie Marie Wade, *Skirted*
Miles Waggener, *Superstition Freeway*
Fritz Ward, *Tsunami Diorama*
Camille-Yvette Welsch, *The Four Ugliest Children in Christendom*
Amber West, *Hen & God*
Maceo Whitaker, *Narco Farm*

www.ingramcontent.com/pod-product-compliance
Lightning Source LLC
Chambersburg PA
CBHW080225170426
43192CB00015B/2759